ISBN -13: 9798812384852

Published by Deborah J. Kelly

Cover Design by Deborah J. Kelly

Formatting and Layout by Maryam Nawaz

www.deborahjkelly.com

DEDICATION

For my inspiring and beautiful Mother

Even in the darkest of times, your love shone brightly enough for me to find my way out. Your patience, acceptance, understanding, generosity, never-ending encouragement, and support always lay waiting for me, to find in myself what only you could see.

For that, I am eternally grateful XX

In Loving Memory – For my wonderful Dad

This book is dedicated in memory of my dearest loving, Daddy. Although you are missing from the memories of my future, your light was so bright it continues to shine on from our past. Thank you for being you, my tonic, and my joy. I love you and miss you so much. I wish I could share these moments with you.

Love as always, your DJ, your Pumpkin, and Kiddo XXX.

CONTENTS

PREFACE

In the mid 2000's my dad died suddenly; a year later I ended an engagement; a few months after that I went in search of meaning and found my Self along the way! In that time, I was given sign after sign that the Universe wanted me to write a book. I would meet random strangers while backpacking and they would later say to me 'Wow, you should write a book', or 'There's a book in you', or 'If you had a book, I would love to read it!'. There are only so many times you can keep hearing it before you must start paying it some attention.

After I arrived home from traveling the world Solo, having found what I was looking for; I went to an incredible Astrologer, here in Dublin. She was able to tell me events in my chart which had already come to pass, and she spoke about events which I could expect to find opportunity in. She then asked me when was I going to write my book? 'How the heck do you even know about that!', I thought? She said it as though we had conversations about it before, as though it was already done or in progress. I explained that I had many signs telling me to write a book, but I had no idea what about. I had some ideas, but none which I felt comfortable with. It was around this time I was already planning another trip away, to the Camino. My Mum offered me to go to a Hay House Writers Workshop in Dublin the same weekend I was planning to go on the Camino, so I declined. The tickets were expensive and not something I would have bought for myself; I hadn't yet accepted I was a writer, and it was all still a little bit of fantasy. The idea of being able to write a whole book seemed like a mountain I wasn't sure I wanted to climb. But once again, the Universe was not giving up on me, and even my Mum could see there was something written in the stars. On a weekend away I injured my feet, and this meant my Camino trip was no more. My Mam decided to buy the tickets for Hay House, so we went along.

That weekend was the most intensely bizarre experience! I was watching the Universe act in real time! The opening video came on, as we all settled ourselves in our seats, and the video said: 'There is no better time to write a book, than now!'. I felt overwhelmed with emotion and cried silently to myself. It was strange, as though it took me by surprise. Something really struck a chord with me! A writer called Robert Holden, was a guest speaker at the workshop. He got up on stage and asked us all to write a small paragraph starting with 'I write because....'. He gave us 5 minutes and then picked one person randomly, from each seating section, to read their piece. He chose me. I read out loud, shaking at the idea of my inner world being spoken aloud, everyone hearing my depths and words. I had always journaled, written poems and small pieces but never shared it publicly. The microphone shook in my hands as I spoke my words. When I ended, the room erupted in clapping. 'Wow' I thought. I reddened. Robert said, 'I had a story to share' and 'I owed it to my ancestors to share it'! 'What the heck did that mean?' I wondered. But it stayed with me. After Robert, a local Irish celebrity called Bressie, came on stage. He was also as a guest speaker. He was doing a talk about mental health, the darkness we suffer silently, and I cried again. Everything he said resonated so strongly with me. The darkness, the not fitting in, the sadness and lack of confidence. The unspoken words that each of us needed to let out to be free. I cried and knew there was something more happening within me. There was a shift.

That whole weekend I kept meeting random strangers who purposely came over to speak with me. One woman came to me, outside the bathroom, to tell me she loved what I had written and how I spoke. Another woman came over to me and my Mum to say she would love to read my book – even though I hadn't yet written anything! Another woman came over to me while I was grabbing a water and said, 'Oh! It's you! I wanted to talk to you and tell you that your words touched my heart! I can't wait to read your book!' I was floored. It was nuts! If ever I needed a sign that I was meant to write a book, it seemed this was it. At the very end of the weekend, just as we were waiting for the crowds to leave, a woman came up to me and gave me her business card. She was the commissioning editor of Hay House UK and said if I didn't have time to write for their competition, I should contact her as soon as I had my book started or done. I was blown away! I knew there and then I needed to write a book.

Over the course of the following year, I did everything I could to avoid writing the book. I visited the Astrologer again, and once more she said, 'Is the book finished?'. My stars were showing opportunities for communications and publications. I have, over the years, been told time and time again from Shamans, Mystics and Psychics and alternative Healers that I have an incredible light and energy within; that I would not be able to hide in the shadows anymore and I had a role to play. I was to be seen publicly, and I wouldn't like it because I preferred the side-lines. I was told many times I would be successful and not to fear following my path; that my Ancestors were waiting for me to speak the truth they never could. This all began to make sense to me. I was petrified and it felt horribly uncomfortable, but I had been in search of meaning and wasn't likely to shut the door in its face, if this was it.

In honesty I avoided writing this book. In fact, I tried to come up with lots of other ideas on what I could write about. Deep down, however, I knew this was the one, it had to come out. In a way, I needed to write it to clear the decks for what's to come: for the books that need to be written after this. Since finishing this book, the next book has already begun. The labour pains are threatening it to be written. It's like a wild animal, coming closer and closer. I have the idea, yet I can't see it clearly, but we are getting comfortable with each other. It's letting me know it's there to be written. Funnily enough, it won't give itself to me until this one is finished. As soon as this book was nearly finished, I could see myself running away, distracting myself with other things. I could see how I was avoiding finishing it off at all costs because that would mean I had to decide whether I would publish it or not. What made me not want to publish? With every sharing of the truth is the risk of fallout and destruction of many relationships. However, I have had to carefully weigh up the pros and cons. I always swore to myself, if I could ever find a way out of the pain I experienced, I would share it with other women. This is my book, for them.

My truth caused a lot of pain many years ago and pushing it to one side allowed everyone to move on. I am aware I am opening it all up again. Here I am standing in front of everyone, taking the risk of once again being rejected for speaking my truth. As a kid I didn't have that choice and I silenced myself. As an adult who now knows and understands the role of the abused; they are always the one who suffer in silence. We choose to come to this earth and have a set of experiences; the people we meet along the way are part of that journey. I blame nobody for what happened in my past; I believe that we have soul contracts we come into this world to fill and there is a lesson in everything. I believe and feel I have done justice in conveying my perspective and understanding for everyone's situation; it is the only way to be fair for all involved. I just ask those who feel conflicted in reading this book: be objective. When not emotionally attached to the story it is possible to feel compassion for the protagonist; however, when there is attachment there is fear, and fear of blame, guilt, and feelings of misunderstanding. This book is a means of me writing my truth and allowing my story to help others who have felt unheard, who are looking to find themselves; to help those who are lost, find hope in a way back home to themselves. These books are intended as a tool for healing - therefore: - if you want your world to stay the same and not look at any other perspective, then you should not read this book. However, if you choose to be open to the concept of there being several perspectives and views, and a new way of experiencing life, of understanding we all have our own journey, then please go ahead, and read this book, and/or all 3 books.

To media, or anybody who wishes to discuss the book, I will advise, in advance, this book is meant to resonate with those who feel they have lost themselves on their journey through life. It is meant as a means of showing how lost you can truly be in yourself, yet the soul always wants you feel peace; it always wants you to find your way home. Even the darkest emotions are guideposts back home. The heaviest of emotions are there to make you ask yourself questions, tough questions, and to keep exploring and discovering so you can find your way back. I had to surrender and lose myself completely before I was ready to find myself. When I did, it was as though a door opened. Life is a journey and I admit I don't have all the answers. I am still discovering and exploring; as long as I breathe, I will continue to do so. I will get it wrong, and I will get it right. I will fall off the wagon and lose contact with my inner guidance, and I will come back to it. But now that I know what it feels like to find it, I can never be truly lost: just temporarily misplaced.

To those reading this book, who are thinking of writing their own stories and would like to write their own book... DO IT! It has been the single most therapeutic and empowering thing I have ever done. In truth, the book wrote me. What I discovered as I began to write (not knowing the true direction it was taking) was that my body shook, and shivered, trembled, became cold and agitated as I wrote certain parts. I saw myself intentionally avoid sitting to write. I saw myself get up and down 20 times before writing certain parts. I procrastinated for weeks on some parts. In the end, it was only the starting which was the most difficult. When I was in the flow of writing, it was like therapy. The thoughts were worse than the reality of writing itself.

I grew so much from being present with myself through the process; seeing how my mood changed at just the thoughts of sitting down to write the most difficult parts. My body was once again protecting me. I literally felt as though I went through PTSD while writing some parts of this book. My body released emotions. My mind was clear and focused. I was present and calm. All the while my body reacted in ways I couldn't have ever imagined. While my mind was clear, I saw my own moods shift and change for 'no reason', but of course it was release of emotions and stuck energy.

In the journey through writing this book I felt as though me and my body became better acquainted. I saw how it has so often reacted, in terribly subtle changes, and ways to tell me that I feel uncomfortable; even when my mind feels clear. I have begun the journey of getting to know myself, and it is never too late for anyone to do the same.

Growth is about accepting the light and dark side of life: the light and dark sides of ourselves. It is about seeing that both the light and dark are born from the same place; they are merely signposts and lessons which helps us to grow. Yes, there are tough lessons we go through in life, but there is always something to be learned. The Universe will never give us anything we can't handle. We have all survived every challenge we have ever met, to date.

While on a spiritual path or road of self-development I can say with certainty that I will learn many lessons; I will forget as many, then re-learn them, re-apply them, and continue to grow. There will be some days where we may feel as though all our hard work has been undone. On other days we feel we are fully through the other side of it. Then, something small triggers us and there we are back again with old emotions and triggers. What's important is to be present and patient with ourselves, in the same way we would with a child. Have compassion, love and understanding. These are the most beautiful parts of being human. We are never perfect. We all make mistakes. We all have our own stories, and we all have our darkness as well as our light. It is accepting these parts of ourselves and others; by not being afraid to look at these parts in ourselves and others; by not avoiding and feeling fearful of how these things may change us or others; and holding space, that allows us growth.

I asked a friend of mine, Erica, recently if she had one word for me what would it be? 'You're an Explorer Debs!' she said with such beautiful wonderment and enthusiasm! So, I endeavour to always forge my way through life like an intrepid explorer of the body, mind, and soul.

I truly hope this book inspires you; shows you how, even though all of life's ups and downs, there are lessons to be learned which make us stronger in everything we do. We are all on our own unique paths and ultimately, we are all just trying to find our way back home. We are trying to find our way back to ourselves and the light within. In doing so it may not be perfect, it may not happen immediately and when we want it, but it will happen when its right. We may temporarily lose ourselves along the way, and that's okay; it's part of the journey. When we learn to reconnect with that little voice within and learn to tap into what feels right and wrong for us in our world; to live through our hearts more than our minds, we learn and understand that what feels right inside. What's right for one, may not be the same for another; we can celebrate our differences with love and respect. If not, then there is a lesson in that by itself and all it is, is another signpost leading you back home through another path.

Finally, I hope if you feel you have received some healing, wisdom, or insight from these books, that you will share them with your friends, loved ones and family. I would also love to know how they have inspired or helped you on your journey. Stay connected with Deborah J. Kelly on Social Media or online & Join her Newsletter on www.deborahjkelly.com. Love and Light, Deborah J. Kelly XXX.

***

Coming Home To Me

A Journey of Getting Lost
and Coming Home to Me

Part I: Losing My Self

CHAPTER ONE

PRIMARY SCHOOL – YOU'RE FIRED!

Although I was a child of the 80's my Primary School, an early 19th century single story building, seemed like something from a black and white war movie. It was cold and hard, with 2ft thick walls. The high ceilings and tall plate-glass shutter-style windows allowed hardly any light through. Only illuminated flecks of floating mould and mildew particles could be seen as they caught beams of short-lived sunlight, a rarity in Ireland! Everything smelled dusty and the desks were old-fashioned just like the teachers, and the teaching. They were the type of desks with the built in flip-up seats, ink wells for dipping quills in and shelves below for books, which usually became stuck to the hardened chewing gum hidden beneath! There was often a smell of dead mice rotting which I imagine had something to do with the holes in the old timber floor. Everything about this old school felt hard, rigid, and old fashioned. However, despite my many early years of being bullied here, I quite liked our old school. It had character and I guess part of me felt sorry for its hardened unloved state. To me it was alive and I sympathised with how unseen its beauty was in peoples' minds. Much like how unseen I had felt in my own early years there.

As a kid from a little country village in the South East of 1980's Ireland, my classroom was small and made up mostly of rural class girls and just one or two boys. There were seven of us in total. The boys did their own thing and had nothing to do with us, and the girls all got on great together, except with me. They all disliked me. I was different in some way to them. I couldn't see how, except that I had a skin condition called eczema all over my hands and legs, which often meant wearing bandages to school. They didn't really understand the bandages, but equally I never remember them asking me about them. I just remember them telling me, during games, they couldn't hold my hand or touch me. They never said why, but just looked at me dismissively and that was it.

Outside in the yard at playtime, we would stand around in a circle. Playing 'Ring a Rosie', everyone would hold hands together, except with me. They would say very directly to me, 'I can't hold your hand'. This statement was usually accompanied by a look toward my hands or legs. They often managed to exclude me very simply with these open-ended sentences. Closing down my invitation to be the same as them, they would charm their mastery of pointed looks and body language; which said more than words ever could at that young age.

I remember, the girls would fall out with each other at times. They would then come and ask me if I would like to be their replacement friend. In hindsight, I am pretty sure this was done just to irritate their other friend; yet it filled me up like a doughy-eyed puppy! Without thought or agenda I would, of course, offer my heart open to feel accepted and be one of them, to be included. It usually came with a catch though: there was a time limit depending on how long their fall-out lasted. As soon as they were back friends again, my services were rendered surplus to requirements. I would be back on the bench – once again made redundant. This was just another silent but deadly learning experience. I would have to learn it over and over and over again in my Primary school years, with these girls. The push and pull of friendship. Being invited in one minute and shoved back out the next. There was no consistency to it, other than knowing it wouldn't last. This was one of my earliest memories of the fickleness of friendship; one which would cast its shadows well into my adult life and take me some time to understand.

Of course, at the time I was oblivious to this. I just saw that briefly somebody accepted and wanted me. It would be offered: 'I'm not friends with Marie anymore, will you be my best friend instead?', and that was it. A simple interview question which of course was answered without a second thought by me: 'Yes!'. We would play, as though suddenly, my sins had been forgiven; the ugly grime which they all disliked so much about me had been washed away. I could be seen for me, or at least that's how it felt. However, with this friendship came great trepidation and politics. The fall-out, of course, included some side-taking by all the girls. This never usually rubbed off on me considering none of them liked me anyway. I just followed the lead of my new friend. She would advise me on who we could, and could not, talk to. In a matter of days, and usually more like a few hours or a single day, I would hear the dreaded sentence from my new best friend, 'I can't be your friend anymore because me and Marie are back friends again', and that was it. No more explanation or warning, it was a simple 'You're Fired!'.

I don't remember this affecting me mentally so much back then. I have quite factual memories of all of this, which I feel was my way of coping with it. I removed the emotion. Upon being fired from my position I remember being allowed to maintain my post as a friend for the remainder of the day - or possibly even the following day – as a courtesy. However, I was gradually pushed back out of the circle soon after, once again. Very quickly, all backs were turned. This would happen most noticeably by my being included in group games like 'Tag' or 'Hide and Seek'. Then afterward being told I wasn't allowed play. Again, there was usually no explanation only open-ended toneless statements, and those looks. Those fatal looks which pointed me off to the distance, as a hint to be anywhere else they weren't.

At times when I was included; I would be allowed to borrow a pencil, ruler or sharpener during my time within the inner circle. This was a sign you were accepted into the pack. However, after being fired I would soon be reminded of my position. I would no longer have the privilege or access to borrowing stationary. I'd ask one of the girls for a pencil and be declined. The 80's and 90's were all about having every type of stationery under the sun, it made you pretty cool! As I looked at a full pencil case, with a huge array of stationery inside, I would be met with a vacant steely that said 'I don't have anything you can borrow!'. Again, these words which said very little and silently spoken by looks, said it all: I was out. No longer part of the group, it would only take one of them to un-accept me for them all to then say 'Sorry, I can't be friends with you anymore'.

On some occasions I felt a little sadness in their eyes. Sometimes, my inclusion in the group was fun and I was liked. However, as soon as one decided I was not to be liked anymore, they all had to follow suit and begin to ignore me. Even when I felt that perhaps some didn't want to. It was odd really because, looking at this as an adult, it's incredible the psychological warfare and maturity of their skills together as a pack. It's truly impressive really at that age.

I remember on one occasion, sitting in the classroom during our lunchbreak. There was nobody but us in the room. The girls were speaking about something funny, which made them giggle. I was part of the included gang at this stage, or certainly was on the edge of it. When I asked what they were talking about I was told they couldn't tell me. Again, they excluded me as a pack. They said if I wanted to know I needed to ask Mrs Cathbert, the teacher. So, I did!

Mrs Cathbert came back into the room after lunchtime. The room hadn't yet filled up. As the girls continued to giggle - now at me - I went up to the Teacher's old worn wooden desk which had been varnished so many times the actual colour of the desk was hard to tell. It sat in front of a huge dusty old black chalkboard. I told her 'The girls won't tell me what they are talking about and they told me to ask you. They won't tell me what a 'Condom' is!'. I said this with absolute innocence. I have a vague memory of Mrs Cathbert being very cross with me for asking about such a thing: she was pretty angry with me. It was 1980's Catholic Ireland after all and any mention of sex was taboo! Just as this happened, I also remember looking back at the girls. I could see their fear and shock. They hadn't realised I would tell the teacher it was they had sent me to ask the question! It had backfired!

I imagine they had hoped I would just ask the question, not mentioning them or why I was asking, and then land myself in it! Of course, this meant I was no longer in or even on the edge, I was exiled again!

***

CHAPTER TWO

FRIENDS & FAMILY – OPEN/CLOSED DOOR POLITICS

Every now and again, when one of the girls were secretly friends with me, I would bring them home to my house after school to hang out. This rarely happened, and without any consistency; not only because they would have to be friends with me for it to happen, but my Dad (who was a Policeman at the time) was an extremely private person. He hated having our friends back to the house.

I'd just like to take a moment here, to highlight something. Although my Dad was my best friend and somebody I could speak to about anything in my adult years, he had two very different sides to him. He flipped from happy to not-so-happy pretty easily; you wouldn't want to be on the bad side! In his older years he actually mellowed out a good bit, however as kids, he was quite different.

Underneath it all he was a big kid himself; had a great sense of fun, humour, and was a hopeless romantic with us as kids. He loved to treat us, to set up games, play hide and seek, leave us surprise notes to say he loved us, send us on treasure hunts, gave us days off school and bring us away for surprise trips etc., for no reason. In fact, I have so many memories of him appearing through our bedroom door early on a school morning singing (more like gleefully shouting) 'I-GOT-THE-POWER!' . This was a nudge to the 1980's song by SNAP called 'The Power'. My Dads way of being intentionally 'UnCool' was by pretending he knew pop songs and sing them all wrong! When we heard this, it was code for 'we didn't have to go to school' and were going on an adventure! He loved a bit of spontaneity.

His flip side I feel was caused by stress and him battling his own demons. This meant he was quite temperamental, easily frustrated and angered. If his mood was off, you made sure to behave and stay out of sight. When we were kids, I feel, he didn't have a great patience or tolerance threshold. It was always something he struggled with, but which was far worse when we were kids.

These frustrations and lack of patience were something I used to suffer with in my own life many years ago. It is something I certainly inherited from him and worked very hard to undo the imprinting I absorbed by osmosis in those early years. It's incredible how much of our Parents' traits, good and bad, we take on early in life. But rather than blame those who went before us, I feel it is up to us to become as conscious as possible of who we are. To recognise what belongs to us and what has been inherited as a program. It is up to our generation to release and forgive the 'Sins of our Fathers' so to speak, as a means of doing for ourselves what our ancestors could not do for themselves. To express, access and release unhealthy emotional patterns. Simply because they did not have the freedom, the education or consciousness to do so, as we have today, for themselves.

I believe that, as kids, in your most formative years you learn to emulate your parents and their traits and habits. It is our way of bonding and forming our personalities. Based on trying out the characteristics we see and hear. With this in mind, what we need to understand is: the same could be said about our parents from their parents, and for their parents from their parents and so on. Emulating and picking up traits and habits', both positive and negative, from those we look up to as kids. This happens generation after generation without being addressed and understood. When it is brought into conscious awareness and released, we can then see - and perhaps understand - just how much family baggage we carry as the generations come and go. Perhaps, in the day and age we live in, it is the responsibility of the current new-age thinking generations to release and transform that baggage. To do this for all those who have gone before. Not for us to blame or see them negatively for these influences we have inherited. But to understand the process and release the blame; for those who were unable to do this for themselves; for our ancestors who never had the tools, understanding, and permission of free-thinking, as we have today. Perhaps our greatest gift, to the generations to come, is to see that we have carried so much pain. To see the hurt through all the generations, and release that with forgiveness. To let it go for all who have gone before us and those who are yet to come.

Now I will come down from my soap box and get back to the story! Essentially, we all have our good and bad sides. We inherit a lot but it's up to us to uncover what belongs to us. Then leave the rest behind.

In the mid 1990's, my Dad retired early from the Police Force due to severe stress and bullying. I remember all the trips to the Police Headquarters in Dublin. I remember him always telling us, as a kid he had always loved Hypnosis. He watched stage shows in his local theatre. Anything to do with alternative thinking, psychology and the mind, he and my Mum had an interest in. It was therefore no surprise to those who knew him, when he retired, he became a Hypnotherapist and Psychotherapist. He even set up his own Clinic, at home, in our house. This was when he really began to come into his own self and he mellowed much more. On becoming a Therapist it is impossible to not grow and develop personally, that's what much of your work grows from. Your mess is your message I guess. I feel this is what helped him settle into himself.

In many ways this example, his stress as a Policeman and mellowing out as a Therapist, is a good demonstration of how life shows us Signposts. If we only knew how to see and read them. I truly believe when we are out of alignment with our Soul purpose, we suffer huge amounts of stress and anxiety. This is our Soul saying 'You're going the wrong way!'. I feel, the perceived 'negative' emotions and feelings usually have gold nuggets of wisdom in them. Albeit its not always so easy to detach from the intensity of an experience to see them. But they are simply signposts, pointing us back home to ourselves. We are meant to be happy as humans, therefore pain and joy is what tells us when we are in or out of alignment. If we could learn to see it this way, we could all learn to find more contentment and happiness in life. I believe, as soon as we are doing that which we were born to do, we find much more peace and contentment in ourselves and in our lives. This is where we experience flow.

With my Dad, it was clear he was born to be a Therapist. He was an incredible source of strength and transformation to hundreds of people in his Clinic. We shared an interest of the mind, body and soul. Anything related to the Human Experience and the countless esoteric talks into the wee hours of the morning, were always up for grabs. When I grew old enough to share a few drinks with both my parents, it was these deep chats that helped us all to bond. I feel, it took me getting older to have those bonding chats with my parents; talking about and pondering on life, people, society and whatever else came up, was what helped me to grow as an individual. Their way of entering these discussions was always over a few drinks. It was how their generation learned to share stories and experiences around the fire. It was these chats that helped the relationship, trust and understanding between myself and my parents develop.

If my Dad was pretty intolerant with us as kids, you should have seen him with other people's kids. He often felt there was a lack of 'manners and respect' in how other kids were reared. He hated us having friends call around to the house without having agreed it all in advance. He hated surprise visits, which we knew all about as kids.

An example of my dad's dislike for surprise visits was: at home whenever we would hear a car come around the driveway. He would run up to the big, tall window on our stairs. It overlooked the back of the house where the cars were parked. He would hide behind the net curtain to see who was driving in. If he couldn't see properly - or at least without the prospects of getting caught - he would go upstairs to our bathroom window. Here he had his second look out point, a small square window behind our cast iron bath. He would lean awkwardly all the way over the bath to look out and down below, to see who was there. If the vantage point still wasn't good here, then there was always the window from my brother's bedroom, across the hall. In hindsight this game was quite funny to watch, and we even laughed about it later-on as adults; but at the time it was very serious business.

My Dad would always want to know from us 'Who is it?' before we could tell the visitor whether "He was in!". This meant if it was somebody he wanted to avoid, which often it was, we would have to lie saying 'Daddy's not in now'. This was a bit awkward because his car would be parked outside. Of course, he was in the next room listening to us inform the unsuspecting visitor. If we felt it was too obvious to the person we would have to say 'Daddy's asleep, he was working nights'. They would drive off and he would be free again.

This hide and seek wasn't limited to in-person callers. We also had the same routine for people who rang our house-phone. We would answer the phone, vet the call to see whether he would take it or not; to see whether 'He was in' and go from there.

We didn't have a house phone until years after everyone else had one. Back then there were no mobile phones, we only had the fixed line, house phone. When I found out we were having one installed in our house I couldn't wait to tell everyone in school! I would be considered 'One of them'; one less thing to be different!

I remember just before the house phone was installed, making plans with the girls in school to call each other. I eagerly gathered phone numbers so we could try out the new phone when it arrived. When the phone was finally installed, I asked Daddy for our phone number. I was told it wasn't to be used by us kids! I remember feeling so much panic! The girls were expecting me to ring them…

How would I tell them I wasn't allowed?! It felt as though my whole opportunity of 'being included' with them was under threat, like my world had collapsed…. It was just another reason for them to not like me. To add insult to injury, Daddy had told us that we weren't even allowed to give our phone number out to anybody either! It was 'Ex-Directory', which meant it was a private number and couldn't be looked up in the Phone Directory or Yellow Pages. He said, we needed to keep it private. So of course, as soon as the girls asked me about the phone, I had to say I couldn't ring them. They all jeered at me and told me I must have made the whole thing up. They didn't believe I had a phone at home at all. So, later when I did invite friends round to the house, I was always relieved when they saw the house phone in our hallway. It was a kind of proof I hadn't been lying. In honesty, I don't even think it mattered to them. It was just another way to exclude me.

Because my dad was a Policeman, this was another reason to exclude me. He knew a lot of the criminals in the local area and to me it sounded like most families where we lived, in a rural part of Ireland, were mostly criminals. Or at least that's how he made it sound to us, though they weren't.

He didn't like the kids from school coming to the house because he felt they would be 'going home telling their parents' all about our house; it would invade his privacy. He felt the parents were nosey and would talk. I often wondered what it was exactly they would be bothered talking about... my friends were there to spend time with me and not be bothered with him, but in some way, I felt he thought they were like little mini spies!

My Mam, on the other hand, loved when I would bring friends home. I imagine she could see how hard it was for me to make friends and would be overjoyed at the thought that I would bring somebody home.

Later in life she told me, when she was a kid, they had an open-door policy to her home in Leitrim. A small county in the midlands near the west of Ireland. She grew up, the eldest of ten on a farm which also had a shop. The door to their house was literally always open to any passers-by. That's all she wanted for us. To have our friends over any time we wanted. Her open-door policy was very different to my Dad's, so Mam was always the one to ask if we ever wanted to have friends over. My Dad's childhood was a little different and I can see how it caused conflict between the two of them, when it came to allowing friends stay.

My Dad was the youngest of four, the only boy. He grew up over a B&B and worked serving their customers from a young age. He always expressed his difficulty, and the complicated relationship he felt he had, with his parents. He often felt misunderstood, unaccepted, and even attempted to run away from home on many occasions. His Aunts, Uncles and Neighbours were not often surprised to find him on their doorstep. I guess his want for privacy in later life, having a secure and private space which was his own and not invaded by others, was therefore important to him. He liked certainty and to be in control of that. My Dad was a sensitive soul, empathetic and craved love, and acceptance his whole life.

My Mum, on the other hand, although she was the eldest and essentially helped to rear her siblings and work the farm, she too had a tough upbringing. A lot of responsibility was placed on her shoulders at a young age. There was not much time for her being a kid; however, she felt loved, had lots of loving family and friends and got on well with her parents. Her house always welcomed everyone. Passers-by ducked their head under the short doorway of her cottage home, my Granny's house, and called in any time of the day or night - the door was literally always open.

No knocking on the door was ever really expected in my Granny's house. In fact, my memories in childhood were of people faintly rapping a knuckle on the glass pane of the door as they passed the threshold and walked right in. Their knock was less of a question and more of a statement. With a kind of 'Hello I'm here' on their face as they came straight into the front room. Whether it was neighbours, family, or family of family there was always somebody dropping in to say Hello.

I feel, looking at both my parent's childhoods, that people back then had a great sense of community and looking out for each other. Welcoming passing strangers, putting people up for the night, callers to a home were not unusual. I certainly can say this was not the case in our house. We had a closed-door policy, unless vetting in advance with plenty of warning and notice of arrival was given! That's not to say it never happened. More to say it wasn't always immediately welcomed! When my Mum was in charge and Daddy was working shift work, the 'closed door' always seemed more relaxed, pliable, open, and revolving! That's how we knew to ask Mam when we wanted friends over. I guess every child knows which parent to ask, and they learn this at an early age.

Mam played the Hide and Seek game just a little less than my Dad. Most of the time when people called around, when Mam was home, we would see them pass by the driveway through the big window in the kitchen. Mam was generally still standing at the cooker or sat at the cream Formica kitchen table smoking a cigarette with her legs crossed skirt falling to her knee, as she did the crossword. I can still see her so clearly, relaxed with her mop of dark hair, and white streak in the front. Her energy calm and nurturing.

Although Mam would generally be unphased by the casual unplanned visit of people to our house, there were still occasions when she would do what we called 'A Daddy on it'! Using his routine of rapidly escaping then pretending to the unexpected caller that she wasn't there or that she was bathing one of the lads or busy for some reason. It didn't happen as often, but one was as bad as the other and knew when to run. There was a pair of them in it. As kids we learned very quickly how to play this game when somebody would call. Me and my two older brothers knew the drill.

On some occasions we got it wrong. We would naturally assume as kids that people they knew, be them family or family friends, were not on the 'suspect list of people to hide from'! Wrong!! It took a few angry attempts but eventually we knew never to assume!

I remember on a few occasions somebody arriving through the back door unannounced (the door was never locked and always ajar) – 'Is your Daddy or Mammy home?' they would say. This was usually a familiar face of somebody my parents knew and liked. So, we would say 'I'll go get them', then skip merrily about the house in search for Mam or Dad. When we found them, we would be told in low whispers, 'Tell them I'm not here', to which we would have to explain: 'Eh, we kind of already said you were here' – Enter catastrophe! The world had ended and we as 'Silly little kids' had unknowingly pushed the big red button! Uh-Oh! Then between Mam and Dad they would have to decide which of them 'was and was not here'. We would pass on their excuse and the poor unknowing visitor, would be sent on their confused but merry way!

I don't believe I ever learned how to ever be completely relaxed at the idea of a spontaneous caller to the house. I grew up never truly knowing what it was like to have somebody arrive to the house and feel relaxed, grateful, and overjoyed. I was always waiting to know if this was a good or bad thing. Always looking over my shoulder for Mam and Dad's reaction. Again, this is something we have all joked about as adults, at how ridiculous it was. But as kids it was nerve-wracking! We were certainly in the making for an academy award, best performance, by the time we reached our teens.

As an adult I love the idea (but not the reality) of friends or family spontaneously calling by and dropping in unannounced, for a chat or cuppa; I have a romantic view of that old-fashioned familiarity. This was once a thing in Ireland, and something you don't see much of anymore. However, in truth, I am quite a private person and like to know when somebody is coming…. And more especially when they are going! I like my space and feel an intrusion to my freedom when imposed upon. I know that sounds awful to some, but I guess it's as though all those years left an imprint. As I said these moments leave their mark and become part of who we are, for better or for worse.

Through the years, I have grown more in touch with myself, my emotions, my thought processes, present awareness of the "Now". I find that I can catch these old thought and fear patterns in their tracks. Once I realise what they are, I can see them as just that… old patterns; and let them go (as best I can). I remind myself they are old records that serve no purpose anymore. It takes practice, and I must remind myself every time, but I'm getting better at it. I've also grown to accept that it's okay to like my own privacy, have boundaries, and not feel bad when these feelings do arise. In Astrology my Moon (inner emotional security and inner world) is in the 4th House (representing Home and Privacy). Which in essence means internally what I need to feel secure in the world, emotionally, is privacy in my own home. Isn't it incredible how much we inherit from our upbringing and yet when we look at our Astrology, it is already written in our stars too?

So, back to the story. As mentioned, we didn't often have friends over. When we did it was always pre-arranged by asking my Mam the day before. Usually, it would be arranged for when my Dad was working, which meant he either didn't have to know or it didn't affect him. There were occasions when I would accidently agree to one of the girls from school coming over, without first okaying it with Home. My mission was then to get this passed by okaying it with Mam! If I asked the wrong parent and got a 'No', having already agreed it with the girl from school, then changing plans would mean total embarrassment.

When my friends did come over, we would play with my toys and dolls or play DJ on the radio, recording ourselves on tape cassette, in my bedroom. If Daddy was at work and it was near 6pm, my ears would be glued for sounds of his arrival home. When I heard the gravel on the driveway outside, below my bedroom window, crunching under the tyres of a car, my friend would have no idea, but I would secretly be absolutely FREAKING IT! If it was near 6pm then it was most likely my Dad home, and he would not be happy to see anyone visiting when he expected to come home and relax without having a stranger in his way! We would continue to play, and I would be listening in the background, my hearing pushing past my bedroom, over the landing, and over the stairs, straining to hear the voice that was to enter the kitchen below... hoping it wasn't him, so we could continue to play with ease! If it was, my stomach would turn and I would feel anxious, wondering what his mood was like. If he was joyful and in good form, he would be fun and pleasant and a joker, even with my friend there. He would even try to impress himself as the 'Cool Dad', fun and playful. If he was in a bad mood then I made sure to keep us out of sight. I tried to keep us to the confines of my room and out of his space. Otherwise it would spell embarrassment and humiliation for me!

I remember one occasion when it didn't go so well; we had an old-fashioned black telephone with a circular dial which was broken and something I used to play with as a toy. Daddy came home early one day, in bad mood. My friend and I would have been playing on the stairs at some point, but we were now in my room. We had left our toys and the black phone on the stairs. Now Daddy was home, I made sure to keep us in my room, hiding. As he walked up the stairs, I'll never forget, he must have hit his foot or stumbled on the phone which lay abandoned from our play. He got so annoyed and went CRAZY! He knew I had a friend over and she was in my room. He clearly felt totally inconvenienced and intruded upon and made me feel it, and aware of it, from my bedroom! He shouted a lot of F- words and gave out crazy about the toy which had been left there; shouting to the air as though nobody was listening, but aiming it at me through the bedroom door. (He often did this: giving out about a person when they weren't there but knowing he could be heard. He would complain to the air about how thoughtless and careless the other person was; how they never thought about anybody else. He would have garbled words of anger and frustration at the inability of us to avoid disappointing him and meeting his expectations). He threw the phone down the stairs; the bell 'binged and bonged', bouncing and clanging on each step. The sound of the plastic handset hitting off the body of the phone as it then separated. I heard it flung into the air and finally smashing against the wall... magically surviving, with a 'D-LING'! How phones back then were made of stronger stuff!! If that was a mobile phone today it wouldn't have survived past the first step of the stairs!

This happened enough times in my childhood; these scenes which hinted at us that we should have known better than to have somebody at home without his knowing; I knew better than to offer people to come over to our house. Because the girls in primary school didn't truly like me, I was never offered to go to their houses; in fact, I don't remember ever being inside the walls of any of their homes. When they did come to my house it was never to be spoken of in school the next day. If I did mention it by saying 'when Mary was in my house...' it would be met with a swift 'No I wasn't !!!' by her and total denial of the event. This was enough to shut down any future discussions of it happening. It was as though being friends with me, outside of school, was a dirty secret. It became an unwritten rule, that if I wanted any level of friendship, it was only to be had in secrecy, privacy, and between me and them. It wasn't to be made public.

***

CHAPTER THREE

GROWING UP, 4TH CLASS – A NEW START!

When I first went into 4th class it meant that I got to move into the big kids' classroom. I would have been around 6 years of age. This room was for the older 4th, 5th & 6th Class kids, with kids aged 10 -12 years in there. So, it meant that we had moved up the mature ladder; we would finally be mixing with the older kids. A lot of the older kids were seen as the rebels and Messer's, doing cool stuff, and getting into trouble. The big kids' classroom often featured at least one of them standing, as punishment, outside the door. Moving into this classroom would bring us closer to the fun, getting a chance to be on some sort of even keel with them, talking to them, and it also meant that I would share my classroom with my Big Brother Pat!

There was only 2 years of age between me and Pat, and two years between Pat and Joe, the eldest. I have so many beautiful memories of our childhood together and I loved my two big brothers so much. I wanted to be with them all the time, doing what they were doing or at least be near wherever they were.

As the youngest and the only girl in the family, I feel so blessed to have had the brothers I had. Pat was only two years older than me and was great for playing with me, even at girlie games. He was a great playmate, really fun and creative and he came up with new ideas all the time. Like the 'Mars Bar' game; where you had to play music and put on a jumpsuit, hat, gloves, scarf, and socks and boots as quickly as possible while the other person took slices and ate a Mars Bar; the aim was to eat the whole bar before the other person finished dressing up! If you were too slow putting all the items of clothes on, there was no chocolate left and you missed out! We were always making or playing something. Whether it was playing in the garden or having competitions over who could make, drink and eat, the vilest concoction of sandwich or drink in the kitchen, when Mam and Dad weren't looking! It was pretty awful! Some Saturdays we would even make breakfast in bed for Mam and Dad together. Poor Mam and Dad, the breakfast was usually rock solid, burned and freezing cold, but they masked their pain well!! While they ate their breakfast, we would sometimes put on a morning Punch and Judy show, using the Puppet Theatre Santa got me. I have great memories of this, and have a vague recollection of us giving Mam and Dad an early morning buffet of sweets and crisps, as they had just woken up in bed and they watched our theatre! To kids, any time of the day is time for sweeties!

Joe, was four years older than me, and was mad into football and music. It was Joe who introduced me to most of the alternative music I knew growing up. He would come into my bedroom real serious, handing me (or should I say entrusting me with) a new Tape/CD or Album he had recently bought or listened to, telling me to listen to it. Alanis Morrisette, The Verve, Stone Roses or Undertones were some of my earlier exposures! I also remember sneaking in, late at night, to listen to his little red radio. He used to listen to a radio-sketch called 'Amelia Go Lightly', on 2FM Radio at midnight. It was controversial political comedy - of course I was too young to understand most or any of it, and I had no idea what she was saying most of the time - but I loved that we shared these small memories and moments together. As he would laugh, so would I – mostly excited by the fun we were having and not the content of the sketch.

Joe would also rarely be seen without a football when we were kids and was always kicking the ball against the side of the house. My Mum would go crazy as it brought down the already loose plasterwork, but we had fun competing against who could knock the next piece off the wall! The higher the plaster came off the better! When there was a big football match on TV, Joe would always drag me to Mam and Dad's room to watch it with him on their little white TV. Wrapping me up in 'Ireland' theme hats and scarfs and teaching me the rules, and how to shout at the TV! We also watched WWF together, and Saturday mornings would be where I'd learn to do 'Clotheslines' and 'Slam Dunk' moves in the hallway, during the adverts! This of course often led to tears, but we all had great fun!

Sometimes we would all play together; I really loved those times! We would all walk or cycle up into the local woods. We would play in the ponds, collecting tadpoles and/or collecting berries. Often, we would go home with our hands and clothes black and blue, from picking blackberries. Sometimes we all played football together around the field at the back of our house; that usually ended in tears! We were all pretty competitive. Around the edges of that field, which was lined with trees, we all had our own treehouses too! Our own section of the field. It was always great fun climbing through, trying to make it around the entire circumference of the field through the trees, to each other's treehouse. I loved growing up with my brothers, and they always entertained and included me even though I was a bit younger than them.

The dynamics as you can imagine was a little different in school together than at home, and it took me a little while to understand that. Because I always wanted to be where my brothers were, I initially couldn't wait to start school. I always wanted to know what it was they did during the day while I was at home. When we were at home it was okay to play together. But when we were in school things were more serious, more separate and we all had our own lives and friends. I don't recall seeing the boys so much when I was in school. Because of the age difference, it meant that when I was in the little baby's classroom, Pat was in the middle classroom and Joe was in the big grown-up classroom down the end of the hall. The grown-up classroom was where everyone wanted to be.

I also remember, when I about 5 or 6, because once again I always wanted to do what the two boys were doing, I tried to pee into the toilet backwards! The boys always peed standing up at the toilet bowl. It confused me as to why they did it that way and I had to sit on the seat, to pee? It wasn't fair, they always got to do it differently to me and I just wanted to be the same…. so, I climbed up on the toilet bowl, facing backward toward the cistern, little legs akimbo straddling the sides of the toilet and tried to pee facing the bowl too! Needless to say, it didn't work very well!

Idolising my two brothers extended into wearing their clothes! Trying to be like my brothers, was my way of feeling accepted and being like them. So, every time they were finished and throwing out a
T-shirt or some other clothes, I would take it and start wearing it. I even wore some of my Dad's old shirts - which I have tragic proof of - on a National Kid's TV show called 'The Works', which I was invited onto while in 4th class. This was a pretty epic fashion fail!

Finishing 4th class was a big deal. It meant it was almost time to make our Confirmation (a religious ceremony). It also meant we only had two more classes (5th and 6th) after that to pass through before leaving our Primary School forever. We would then head off to the big Secondary School. However, for me, when the time came to move into 5th class it was decided that I would be held back a year, repeating 4th class for another year. Although I was in protest and felt my parents must really hate me to do such a thing, I had no control over it. It was so embarrassing. However, it was for my own good. I was quite young starting school and in fact, staying back would allow me a fresh start, new classmates etc.

As a toddler, before I started school, I would sit at the window and wait for the boys to come home. I would watch the footpath outside at 3pm for them to appear and would be so excited. I too wanted to go to school. I wanted to do what they were doing and be where they were. I begged Mammy and Daddy to go, so I started school a little early.

Staying back a class meant I was once again in the same rows of seats, in the same classroom, but with different people, while the rest of girls would all move on. A new bunch of people were going to join our classroom. They seemed young to me. They would be my new classmates and new friends. It was another small class, of mostly girls again so I was a little nervous over the transition.

Before the Summer came and our classes changed over, I knew I had to suss the new class out and see what I was getting into. Being rejected for years with the same people, was far safer than being rejected by a completely new bunch of people! That would be a whole new kind of rejection. Although I had expected it to happen, I didn't know any different at that age and just assumed the next class would be the same; I expected that I would continue to be an outcast. I just didn't know in what way it would happen, so I wanted to know exactly what I was getting into, and one day I confronted it.

I remember it clearly. It was lunchtime in our little Gym Room where we usually ate our Lunches. I saw one of the girls from my new class, Norma. She didn't look too scary to me, in fact she always looked quite quiet and shy to me. I approached her, my heart beating in my chest, and said: "I'm in fourth class and am staying back a year. Would you mind if I was in your class with you?". I'll never forget it. As an adult looking back it seems so sad that I felt I needed to ask permission, and on the other hand it's kind of funny because what choice did she have, really? If she said: 'Yes actually I do mind', then there was nothing I could do about it! I guess I was sussing her out, by being friendly and polite to see whether she would be nice or mean to me, and then I knew what I was getting myself into. Her reply was soft, passive and a little confused; she just said 'No, sure, of course I don't mind!'. I was accepted!

From that moment on I felt a little safer. Come the following school year I began my gradual transition of hanging around with the girls in my old class to making friends with my new class. They all seemed to readily accept me and didn't seem at all put off by me. None of them seemed to be putting any effort into excluding me or making me feel different or in the way. In fact, none of them seemed to even notice my eczema, something central to a lot of the jeering and meanness I suffered from the girls in the past. I just seemed to exist as an entity on my own without having a past; they knew me for me. They knew nothing of my past years in school because they were always a class below and never hung out with us. They didn't even know that the other girls in my class didn't like me, because all the meanness, exclusion and bullying was done so silently and out of view. I had a fresh clean slate to start on. We were all happy, the other girls were finally rid of me, and I had new friends.

I remember, as my transition continued, I could sense the girls from my old class looking over at me. They could see me happy, see me included and having fun with my new friends; they could no longer exclude me, they had no control over me anymore. It wasn't long before they could see how I had moved on and forgotten about them too. I didn't 'see' them anymore, and I think that initially bugged them a little.

A few years later they moved on to Secondary School, as I finished the year behind in 6th class. When the time came for me to move to secondary school, I was a whole new person. I had done a lot of growing in those years, and I had really begun to step into a newer version of myself with a little more confidence. All I needed was the distance between me and them, distance, and space for me to grow. It's hard to grow when you are suppressed every day. Something I would realise once again in later life. When you spend more time trying to see yourself through other people's eyes; trying to constantly figure out why you have been picked on, rejected once again, or understand what's wrong with you, it's hard to see yourself from your own eyes.

When you are constantly trying to be one step ahead of rejection, and one step ahead of the game, it's hard to grow. In fact, it's impossible to grow when your attention is always outside yourself and not on yourself. Sometimes it's only when you step away from the very situation that's suppressing you, from the distraction and pain, that you really thrive and grow. But knowing, in the first place, that you need to step away is the most difficult part. I felt safer with the girls I had been bullied by for years, because it was familiar, and the very idea of change terrified me. I was afraid of more rejection. However, thanks to my parents for removing me from that class, those girls and those situations, later in life I would see the benefits of change. These years were to be a life lesson, which was integral to my growth, but which took me well into my adult years to realise and understand.

Interpersonal Relationships, trust, vulnerability, and being alert to manipulation, have always been a tenuous thing for me. In fact, many of my interpersonal relationships, through the years, have contained some element of learning to be aware of these challenges. As an empath and highly sensitive person I find the good in everyone and therefore have easily fallen into manipulative and narcissistic relationships throughout my life. For the most of my adult life I had been asleep to all of this. Still to this day, even with the knowledge and growth I have had, I sometimes need to remind myself this is a work in progress. Becoming okay with this ongoing growth has been the kindest reward and gift I could have ever given myself. Educating myself to the various challenges I have faced, and understanding the psychology of how people, and their minds, operate has helped me tremendously. Studying Astrology has also been a help to me. It has always been of interest; however, in the more recent years I have found its accuracy overwhelming and a great help in charting the course of my life; becoming more clear on who I am, my purpose and challenges I can expect along the way. I believe that everything happens for a reason. I can now see how all of this has influenced the work I do.

As an Holistic Therapist and Intuitive Coach who uses Astrology*, Practical Tools and Intuitive Guidance to help women uncover their true selves, reconnect with their inner wisdom and come home to themselves, my journey had led me here.

*As a side note, a wee break from the book, and for those who are interested in Astrology; I have a Virgo (down to earth, practical, analytical and love being of service to others) Sun, Scorpio (truth seeker, detective, and solver of mysteries) Ascendant and an Aries (spontaneous fun loving, impatient and impulsive pioneer) Moon. My Birth Chart Ruler, Pluto (planet of transformation, intensity, power, life, death and rebirth) is in my 11th house of Friendships and Groups – along with cranky old Saturn (planet of Karma, restrictions, hard work and life lessons) hence the life lessons and challenges I have faced within groups and friendships. My Chiron (wounded healer) and North Node (life direction and mission) are in the 7th House of Relationships, which is in Gemini (who is a communicator and gatherer of facts). My Virgo Sun and 7th house ruler, Mercury (planet of communication), is in my 10th House of Career and I have a Stelium (collection or emphasis of planets) in Sagittarius (the teacher, philosopher, wisdom keeper and searcher of meaning and purpose)...

What the heck does all that mean? Why the heck do I need to know all that - I hear you say!!

Well you don't need to know... But it's really just to show you how Astrology can show us who we are. It can point us to our path and show us how to use our wounds to help others. So, for me, it's pretty beautiful to see how all of my experiences and wisdom gathered have led me to writing a book about my pain, delving deep into the past, as a means of using that wisdom and understanding to help others... it is literally already written in the stars!

Therefore, it makes so much sense to me now, that my early childhood experiences and difficulties which left such indelible marks on my soul, would include relationships and communication, and for me to share that wisdom. This would, in turn, be the very aspect of my personality and life which I needed to place the most focus on improving. So, no matter how crappy your past has been, it has been for a purpose and will serve you somewhere in your adult years. I read many charts for people, in the work that I do, and can see this all the time. I can see the hurt, pain, the wounds, and experiences which have influenced who people are... what's comforting to know is, it was meant to be, and it was meant as a means of making you a stronger more resilient you... you just need to find the meaning, for yourself, so you can apply that to your own purpose and mission in life.

I still struggle from time to time with some aspects of all these life lessons. I often need to learn some of them over and over, almost as reinforcement. It's as though I were receiving refresher tests and pop-quizzes from the Universe to keep me alert and awake. But I am getting better at seeing and sensing the energy of these events. I am learning more and more how to establish healthier boundaries and how to say 'No'. Learning it is okay to grow, change, and become stronger in my own self has allowed me to move forward on my journey. Seeing and understanding that we are all on our own unique path through life has helped me to release the need to be accepted. It doesn't mean I am immune to it. It does rear its ugly head from time to time, but my awareness has helped me cope and navigate the challenges with much more ease. As we change and grow, so must our relationships. Understanding that these come and go also has been a huge life lesson for me. I believe we come into this world having made soul contracts with those we love. They have agreed to fulfil the role of mentor and with whom we learn our greatest lessons from. When these lessons have been learned, and we have outgrown the need for these soul contracts, knowing when its time to let them go is important. Therefore, in the last number of years I have let go of many relationships I felt were no longer serving me, or them, on this journey.

Those of you who have had similar experiences may notice you have attracted the same situations or people, into your lives over and over; and the main reason for this, I feel, is because somewhere deep down we haven't become aware, and made conscious, the lesson which needs to be learned. If you are unaware of the lesson, then you will keep getting it over and over until you have mastered it. Much like in school, when you need to repeat a subject you haven't yet mastered. The lesson usually being something we haven't fully processed or interpreted, in us, usually from our early years. You are attracting the same people because you haven't understood 'why' you are attracting them. Like attracts like, and there is something in that person or event which is offering you an opportunity to heal something, own something, reclaim something, or strengthen something in you. Each time you get the lesson on repeat, in a different format, the universe is saying 'Ok, so here's a pop-quiz, a spot test, an opportunity to see have you truly got it... do you truly understood the growth, do you understand what it means to recognise x,y,z'... be it a narcissist or manipulator, boundaries, co-dependency, trust, intimacy, vulnerability etc? Have you learned to know yourself, to see yourself, to know your blind spots or weaknesses which are calling you to be made stronger? Have you learned to interpret your world by becoming more aware of who you are? Have you established your boundaries, and do you know who you are?' I feel these experiences as a kid were in order for me to progress and grow in this life. Knowing this makes things so much easier; however, it doesn't mean that I don't still feel the pain of these years. All it means is that now I am aware of the effects, I can be more present and let the old records come and go with more compassion and less victimisation. I feel more empowered and less dis-empowered.

When we see the world around us as a means of learning lessons, as life experiences that we choose coming into this world - these soul contracts; then we can let go of the victim role and empower ourselves. If we could understand, that on some level before we came to this world, we chose the lessons; we could see them as our own doing and our own choice and therefore feel as though it's all part of a bigger picture. Then perhaps we could let go of our past more easily. However, it's easier said than done and not all lessons are as easily taken and understood. I know this only too well. Some are a lot more painful than others, and more challenging to interpret as we will see in the next chapter.

***

CHAPTER FOUR

FAMILY DYNAMICS

In the Summer of 1987, at the age of 4 years, I had another experience which altered the course of my life. As you will see, in the next chapter, my world would forever shift and adjust to a new normal. It would take me most of my life to go through the motions of this event; to dis-entangle and separate my hurt and pain from that of others; to dis-entangle my emotions and understand how the strands of this event affected many aspects of my life; to finally see my own story without guilt or shame; to find myself and learn to reconnect to my inner voice. It would take years for me to take back my own story and feel my own pain, without guilt. This would be the Summer where I eventually, subconsciously learned (right or wrongly), that telling my truth caused rejection and caused exclusion. Telling my truth caused me to doubt my inner voice and my own instinct; it separated me from feeling, trusting, or knowing my own right and wrong. It confused me and led to the gradual detachment from my inner self, my inner knowing, disconnected from my inner wisdom. It was when I learned that following my inner voice, got me into trouble and made lots of people fall out. It made lots of people look at me differently. I learned to sense emotions in a room before anybody spoke. I learned to sense, in seconds, if somebody liked or didn't like me. I would sense their mood and agenda. I learned that by simply being myself, this was what other people didn't seem to like about me. My presence often seemed to make others uncomfortable, and I just never seemed to fit in anywhere, except at home with Mam, Dad, Joe, Pat and our animals. I would learn to ignore and pretend my past never happened in order help others feel more comfortable. It would help them so they could 'get on' with life. It was something which would take me most of my life to adjust to and recover from.

At the age of 4, in the Summer of '87, my world changed. 'After all, we were all just kids', people would say dismissively in order shut down and put away uncomfortable thoughts of what happened. It made them feel uncomfortable; it was the 80's and people didn't seem to know how to handle these things back then; but while everyone turned a blind eye and pretend it didn't happen, I was left with the life adjustment!

I was 4 years of age just before I started school. We spent the Summer holidays in Leitrim, just as we had done most, if not every Summer before that. My Mum would pack our bags, for myself Joe and Pat. We would take the train, waving goodbye to Daddy at the station. He had to stay home to work. We would get the train from Wicklow to Dublin, then change in Dublin and get the next train to Leitrim. The trip seemed like it took days, and back then would have certainly taken the best part of 5+ hours. We would have stayed a week or maybe two or three, so were well settled there. I loved going to Leitrim, as we had a huge family of cousins, aunts and uncles on my Mother's side.

On my Dad's side he had three older sisters, Joanne, Maureen and Mandy, which meant we only had a handful of cousins.

When we were kids my Dad unfortunately fell out with his family. I remember when we stopped visiting, seeing or even being able to talk about my Dad's parents - my Grandparents - they had such a big falling out. My Dad, who was creative, theatrical and therefore prone to dramatic effect, spray-painted three big, long iron nails in gold; then he hammered them into the wall just above the entrance to the kitchen door at home. Each nail, he announced to us, was be removed one at a time, whenever there was a falling out with his parents. The nails represented their last three chances and when the final one was removed all our hearts broke. It was done with such sadness and anger. I remember him pulling the last one out. That meant he cut all ties with them, which included their being able to visit us. It meant we lost all contact with them for a number of years.

Many years after that event, I have a vague recollection of my Grandparents turning up as a surprise to my 5th or 6th class Primary School Play. I could see them in the audience and knew they weren't supposed to be there. I was so excited but also remember thinking Daddy is going freak out if he sees them. They would not have been allowed visit in the years previous, since their falling out. I just hoped I would get to see them after the play, in time before they either disappeared or all fell out again! However, this time there was no falling out! They all met and seemed to get along. They all seemed to ignore the fact they hadn't seen each other in ages; they all seemed to ignore the pain each other had caused. This dramatic storm of emotions which had resulted in our years of being estranged from our family, just seemed to be ignored and everyone moved on. It was as though the past vanished and was invisible. This confused me greatly. It went from total fall out and anger, to pretending everything was okay and it was all just business as usual...as though nothing had happened. It was weird, but I was grateful to have my Grandparents and Aunties back, even if there was still a little tension. It was a little awkward because I think nobody knew if it would stay like that or if something would blow again. From that moment, I remember things getting a little better.

These were the moments in my childhood which demonstrated how easily people could choose to ignore the uncomfortable things. Even though you could feel it in the background. As I've said before, it was 1980/90's Ireland. It was pretty old fashioned, repressed, and traditional especially in the countryside where we were. People were not so forward-thinking and certainly the new-age thinking we have nowadays was not commonly seen. The relationship never fully went back to the old ways, it was always kind of broken or strained, ready to snap. But some of the doors were a little more open than before. As you can imagine, although all of this happened many years further into my childhood, it was exactly this family rift on my Dads side that led us to spending most of our summers in Leitrim, with my Mums family.

***

CHAPTER FIVE

LEITRIM – MY LIFE CHANGES

In that Summer of '87, on the train home from Leitrim to Dublin I have a vague memory of feeling I needed to pee and no matter how many times I went to the bathroom nothing came. It would just be a dribble and nothing more.

Mam was trying to mind us all on the train. Every time she would bring me to the bathroom, she would have to bring the two boys too. Otherwise she would have to leave them alone for a few minutes. I was too young to go alone. Anytime the boys needed to go, she would need to bring me. I can imagine having three young kids on a long train ride with tons of suitcases and several toilet stops must have been hard work. On this trip I kept needing to go, over and over. I felt I needed to pee but couldn't. It felt like there was something 'down there'. Mam was getting frustrated with how often I needed to go; she knew it was not like me and just couldn't understand how I would need to go to the toilet again so soon.

When we got to Dublin, we all got off the train, kids, baggage and all. I needed to pee again. She got very cross and angry with me, telling me there was no way at all that I needed to pee again! She was worn out and frustrated after a long journey to Dublin, and we were only halfway home. There was another train to get. So, she found the bathroom and brought me again anyway, letting the boys go into the men's bathroom together. Mam warned them not to talk to strangers and stay together and not leave each other, always petrified something would happen to them while they were out of her sight. All toilet stops complete, we boarded the next train from Dublin to Wicklow. We arrived home very late in the evening, with Daddy collecting us from the train station. Although it would have been late, I have a memory of us unloading ourselves, bags and all, into the house. Relieved that we were home sweet home. Mam sent us all upstairs to get ready to have a bath. Me and the boys sharing a bath together, as we were all still young, and a bath full of hot water was a luxury in our cold 300-year-old home!

There were always fights over who got to sit where in the bath! Each of us wanted the rounded end of the bath and nobody wanted the tap end. Mam made sure to swap us around every bath time we had, to ensure we would all have a go. The next battle between the three of us would be, who got to be last out of the bath! There was always a battle over who could stay in longer, as we all loved splashing about with our toys. This particular evening, I was the last to get out of the bath. I remember Mam lifting my little soaking-wet body onto a towel, on the floor. Here she would towel dry us down, ruffling our wet hair and getting on our PJs (pyjamas), which she had warming up nicely on the radiator.

Our house was very old which meant it was pretty hard to heat up and so it was quite cold at times! Growing up we didn't have a shower in our house, unless you can call a hose pipe fixed to the wall outdoors, a shower. So, we would still have baths as we got older. Not together obviously. But even as we got older Mam used to surprise us with our Jammies (Pyjamas) either on the radiator or wrapped around a hot water bottle, as a surprise wating for us when we got out of the bath. She always did cute and thoughtful things like this.

On this occasion, since I was last out of the bath, she was drying me on my own. As she was drying me, I complained of 'it feeling a little sore' between my legs', 'down there'. She asked me where and I pointed to my little 'pee pee' area. She wondered what was going on as she remembered that I was needing to pee or had the feeling of needing to pee a lot, on the train ride home. I kept needing the toilet and now I was saying it was sore there. Then I said: 'Martin touched me there!'.

Martin was a local kid, from the small rural townland where my Mum's family grew up, in the countryside, in Leitrim. He spent most of his time in my Granny's house, kind of like an adoptive son, so to speak. He was one of those kids who just always seemed to be around. Therefore, he became part of the family. Everyone just accepted him in and saw him as just another one of the cousins, although he was a little older. He would be seen hanging out after school, or on holidays, or any occasion he could, to avoid being at his own home. His parents fought a lot. He was quiet and everyone seemed to like him, including me and my brothers who would all play together when we were up for the holidays.

Needless to say, Mam was a bit surprised by what I said. So, she asked me a whole series of questions over what had happened, which I answered. Martin had warned me it was our 'secret'. He told me I would get into a lot of trouble if I told anybody. So, I was afraid to tell her and instead crossed my heart the way he showed me to, showing her it was a secret. Children experiment, that's natural and normal; however, this was a 13-year-old boy carrying out explicit acts with a 4-year-old girl at the time. The nature of those acts and what was done, was not appropriate in any way shape or form. It was sexual abuse. Mammy then very calmly dressed me, and brought me into the spare bedroom, which was adjacent to the bathroom, to wait. She then brought in my two brothers and asked me to repeat what I had just told her, to them. Because Daddy wasn't home yet, he was working night duty, and she knew this was serious, she had wanted to see would I repeat the same information to the boys, and I did. Word for word. After telling them what had happened, I told them I had been very frightened and scared. I have a recollection of jumping on the bed, hiding my feelings of awkwardness by playfully jumping up and down like everything was normal. But I knew it wasn't. Mam then explained to the boys what sexual abuse was. She had wanted to make sure they understood and knew about it in case they were ever in a situation which felt bad or felt wrong. My parents were always very open and honest with us as kids, and always gave us what information and explanations they felt we should know or would be able to understand. It must have taken a lot for her to do that, and it must have been a difficult conversation to have with the boys, but she knew how important it was.

Because this situation was different to anything I had experienced before, even though Mam and the boys seemed okay after me telling them, I wondered had I done something wrong. Especially as Martin had made me swear not to tell. He said something bad would happen if I did. So, I worried that something would happen to me or Mammy or the boys, like he told me it would. I was worried that what I had done was wrong and I had broken a promise also.

I can vaguely see my Dad's face after all of this. Although he showed no emotion, and tried to be normal, I could see him holding it back. I could see his heart break. I could see his disappointment. I initially understood this as though I had done something wrong and this thing that happened in some way made him look at me a little differently. I didn't know what that was. I guess his little baby was no longer a baby. He knew how it may affect me in my future, having dealt with abuse through his working as a Policeman, and later becoming a Therapist. He knew the shadows that lay in waiting, the questions I would ask myself later in life. He knew, from his own experience, how this might affect me. He also knew when a child is sexually abused before they have any understanding or sexual awareness, especially before the age of 7, it can alter their entire foundations and sexual understanding of the world. It sexually awakens them much earlier than they can handle, and they see the world differently to other people, who had the healthy opportunity of a natural progression of sexuality.

I remember learning about something called the Oedipus Complex, many years later. I had attended therapy and later studied Hypnotherapy and Psychotherapy, myself. When a child is very young, the first people he or she falls in love with are its Parents. Little boys tend to have a fixation and fall in love with their mothers and little girls usually tend to have a fixation and fall in love with their fathers. Their first true love. Which is why you hear many little children say they want to marry their mammy or daddy when they get older; they don't understand. I remember saying this about my Dad, and I know countless people whose parents have joked about their own kids saying similar. When the child grows up, starts school and begins to socialise and develop their emotions and cognitive skills, if they are not tampered with, that fixation naturally progresses away from the parent and toward children their own age. This is a natural progression as they head toward puberty. When a child is tampered with, before the age of 7 years, that process is disrupted. All perceptions of the world which are acquired at this time, become the fundamental subconscious programmes that shape the life of their character. Before the age of 7, a child's critical 'yes/no, right/wrong, analytical' thinking has not yet been formed. Their brain wave activity is only operating in Delta and Theta. Meaning essentially, they are operating at levels below consciousness; at the same frequencies a Hypnotherapist would attain in their client to re-programme their mind with new behavioural suggestions.

Before the age of 7 children have no filters or the ability to discriminate fully. They are very easily influenced, manipulated, and information fed to a child at this age goes directly into their foundations without question; they are very impressionable. This is why marketing to children is so effective, we see it in our pop-culture all the time now. The Jesuits have a famous saying 'Give me a child until the age of 7 and I will show you the man', i.e. they can be easily programmed. Before the age of 7 a child is laying down the foundations of communication, relationships, trust, and interaction based on how they are responded to; after this age their brain wave activity and understanding of the world moves into a different state. Therefore, any trauma, abuse, emotional disturbances, extreme stress, anxiety and/or sexual activity before the age of 7 can leave long lasting indentations on that person's life. When a child is sexually awakened, before this age, it creates confusion because they are still 'in love with their parent' but now have a different awareness than is normal and they don't understand their emotions. Oedipus fell in love with his mother and killed his father because of jealousy. There comes a distrust of others, interpersonal relationships, confusion of sexual awareness, misunderstanding of the world around them, dysfunctional sensitivities to people, sex, boundary issues, accepting violent or non-acceptable behaviour as normal, inability to discriminate between safe and threatening behaviours, and can affect the child long into their adult life.

As you can see, its lasting effects can be serious. While we all know that children like to experiment and want to look and see what each other child has 'down below', this usually happens with children of the same age who have developed along the same timeline. However, when a child who is sexually awake, in puberty 9 years older, and carrying out explicit sexual acts with a younger child, in my case who is barely out of nappies (diapers), and has no sexual awareness or understanding at all, and is told to keep it a secret or bad things will happen, you can see how this has long lasting effects.

***

CHAPTER SIX

LEITRIM – THE AFTERMATH

My Mother immediately contacted her family; her Mother and Father, Brothers and Sisters and including Martin's parents. She told them what had happened to me. She advised that Martin should never ever be allowed to babysit any of their children while on his own - something which he had done in the past. The reaction was a falling out from her family. Martin had essentially been accepted into the family for years and everybody adored and doted on him. Because he himself had had a tough childhood it meant that my Granny, Grandad, and sometimes other aunts would take Martin in, and look after him as their own. This happened especially when things were turbulent with his parents.

It would have been hard on the family to hear the information Mam shared. Can you imagine hearing that somebody you loved, you saw as family, adored, and fawned over, has done something like this to a toddler? In one swoop, it means that your view of that person will never be the same; your relationship, your memories, your closeness, your trust, your view of them is altered…. in essence going forward everything changes, your relationship must change. That is, if you accept the truth! If you don't accept the truth you get to go back to how it all was before. To sweep it under the carpet and move on. If you don't believe, accept, or even talk about it, well… then maybe it wasn't real? Maybe it wasn't as big a deal. Maybe it wasn't so serious. Maybe the memory will just be demoted to simple child's play. This is unfortunately what happens for most children who are sexually abused. The victim is rarely heard and suffers in silence. It is always the abused that suffers more than the abuser. The abuser is rarely ever exiled, because it disrupts the normalcy of life for everyone. It is most always the abused that must 'get on with it', or 'get over it', pretend it didn't happen and be 'okay' with it. It is the abused that has to ignore their own emotions, feelings and turn up to every function or family event and be 'okay' with seeing their abuser. Otherwise they miss out. It is the abused who has to listen to their abuser's name mentioned in daily life as though 'it never happened'. This denial of what happened, no doubt, helped others feel more comfortable in their return to how things were. However, the truth was always still there in the background. Like a shadow. It was out, but, there was nothing we could do.

In my younger years I did as everyone else did, I put it out of my mind; I tried to forget what had happened. But it was a pretty big life event for me at that point. There were a lot of emotions, fears, and confusions which still hung around me, which I didn't understand; and while others got to move on, I still had to live with it.

The initial reaction to what happened at the time was that people didn't want to believe it and they just wanted to go back to the way things were. To some extent I can see how this happened, there was a severe lack of information about this kind of thing back then. Sexual abuse was not something many people spoke about, and I can imagine how scary it was for all those involved to know it was on their doorstep. There would not have been many support systems in place to deal with this kind of reality. However, in any case the events which unfolded from there on would continue to echo into the future and hold a shadow over us. Unfortunately, it seemed there was also no support for my Mum and Dad either, or for me. No support for what had happened to their daughter, and with the denial from my Mums family, she too was denied in turn.

Or at least, she wasn't believed and therefore it seemed to her that others felt, she or I, must have been telling lies. In essence, it wasn't received well, and this led to a big falling out between Mam and her family.

During the fall out, Martin's mother drove all the way from Leitrim to Wicklow to apologise face to face to my Mum and Dad for what had happened. Finally, some recognition, and from his own Mother...that was huge! She had never denied what happened, she had believed what she was told. This was huge to my Mam and Dad, who felt so alone with all that was going on. In many ways, on learning this as an adult, it gave me a lot of comfort also. The idea that his Mother believed us, and my Mum's family didn't, was a deep wound to bear. My Mum had been like a mother to her entire family, as the eldest of ten she had always looked out for them and practically reared them all, and it was in her own greatest time of pain, when she needed support, that she lost contact with them all. Nobody, from there on, acknowledged or came forward to speak with her about what had happened, none but Martin's Mother.

My Mam's relationship with her Mum and Dad was severed, as a result. It seemed although my Granny didn't believe my Mam, my

Grandad who was babysitting in another room the night it happened, apparently said he felt bad for what had happened. There was little acknowledgement. This no doubt would have created conflict between my Grandparents also, and so the ripple effect was far stretched. My Granny had very sharp words toward my Mum and saw it as outrageous that this boy, her pride and joy, would be accused of such a thing. To her, surely, I must have been lying about what happened. Perhaps it was easier to ostracise me as I was only in Leitrim once a year for a few weeks, whereas Martin practically lived there. It was easier to assume he was in the right and I was in the wrong. It was easier to believe a grown child and assume I would be too young to remember….to assume I was too young for it to affect me. I was young enough that I would just get on with it. Once again, this is pretty typical for children who suffer sexual abuse, especially at a very young age, it is assumed they don't know any different and will just grow up and forget about it. But they don't, not always, and it certainly goes on to affect some aspect of their lives.

It took years before any resolution was reached, the resolution was to move on and pretend it never happened. However, many years later I heard it said: 'Sure, it was probably just innocent children exploring with each other'. Although it felt as a kind of acknowledgement to me, somehow demoting my memory to make it more comfortable for somebody else to handle, frustrated me more. The initial rejection I felt for my story having been denied was bad, but it was much worse to be acknowledged and then simply rubbished in a different way. There was never really any more talk about it, which meant it didn't happen.

But for me, it **did** happen. I remember it, I remember the emotions, the confusion, the fear, the repulsion, the discomfort, the threat, the after-effects; how people looked at me like I was a reminder and discomfort. I remember sensing people's reactions to me. I remember feeling like I had done something wrong, and how people reacted differently to me when I would be in Leitrim, especially if Martin was there. I remember how, after the event, people would say his name around me, talking about him as if to see my reaction, and later as if to try and normalise his name around me... to de-sensitise me. It felt that others didn't seem to care about how I felt with regards to him, they always seemed more- inclined and busy toward normalising things in front of me by talking about him. I felt that every time his name was mentioned, a shudder would go through my body. It was as though they were protecting him from me, rather than protecting me from him. To me, if I knew somebody had been tampered with, sexually assaulted or abused, the last thing I would do would be to mention that person's name, praise or bring him up in conversation. To me, I certainly would ensure they felt safe, secure, supported, and seen by me when that person was in the room. I never wanted attention, all I wanted was to feel safe, seen and supported in what happened.

It was particularly difficult for my Granny, who I loved very much. I knew she loved me, but there was always a stain on our relationship because of what happened. At times I felt she was angry at me for what had happened, and I guess perhaps she was. I remember as a teenager and younger adult, she came to visit us in Wicklow, after my Grandad had passed away. I remember two to three occasions where we were alone and she would mention Martin, firstly to see the reaction but also, I felt it was as a means for 'getting me over' the whole thing. She never acknowledged it and only ever said 'sure that was a long time ago' and 'it was such a shame we couldn't just be friends'. This hurt me, as it felt as though she once again blamed me for the divide, like I was wrong. Like I was disappointing her by keeping up this 'charade', by keeping up this story. It was like she was in denial of the whole thing, and by talking about him in a normal loving manner, it would make the whole thing go away. It would normalise the whole thing. It would be easier for her to just see us getting along together. Like my experience, or the fall out that came with it, was unimportant because I was just a child. *'An unimportant child'*. It was clear how others felt and so I learned to try to act as okay and normal as possible whenever his name was mentioned, or we were in the same room together.

Most holidays spent in Leitrim we seemed to avoid Martin, which was a relief. I usually stayed with my Granny. However as I grew a little older, I had stayed with my Cousin Elaine's family more often, as this helped me to avoid accidentally bumping into Martin.

I remember on one occasion, when I was around 10 or 12, we went swimming in Leitrim with my family. We went swimming with my cousins; my aunt brought us all. When we came back to my Granny's, we all bundled out of the car, soaking wet, still in our swimsuits half naked and running around all excited for the trip we just had. We ran into Granny's house, through the front room where there were people sitting on the couch. I charged on through and went ahead on to the bathroom to have a shower and change my clothes. Halfway through the shower, as I was washing myself, for no reason I just began to panic. I could feel emotions and energy in my body begin to freak out! I didn't know what was happening and then suddenly an image flashed before my eyes: it was Martin.

I realised he was sitting on the couch out front. I realised I had run past him, on the way into the house. I felt vulnerable and naked and completely disempowered suddenly. I worried that he had seen me, especially as I had grown a lot and was underdressed in a swimsuit. I felt ashamed, embarrassed, I felt alone. I felt his eyes on me, like I could feel him on me again. I could feel a darkness on me that I couldn't wash off. I felt threatened and intruded on. 'He wasn't supposed to be there', I thought.

(There was an agreement, between Mam and Granny that Martin wouldn't be around when we were in Leitrim)!

I shouted calmly for Mam from the bathroom, but there was no response. I shouted again, trying to remain calm, but again there was no response from anyone, nobody could hear me! I felt so alone and began to freak out a little! I shouted again, a little more panicked now. I felt like I was going to be trapped in there and wouldn't be able to leave. I was naked and only had a towel to cover me, what if he could see me naked as I passed by the front room to the bedroom? The bedroom where it all happened! I felt trapped and shouted again.

Eventually Mam came, we went to the bedroom and I calmed down. Martin left some time after that completely oblivious to my panic, but I felt he was making his presence known: that he wasn't hiding! That he had nothing to hide! But I did. I just felt like he had control over that situation and was exercising his authority, his control over me, to show me this was his territory. Proving that he could be there present and everyone would be around him, supporting him, not me.

***

CHAPTER SEVEN

MY OWN FALL OUT

Through the years, although we had all ignored it, it never left me. As a young teenager I began to find my voice about it.

Initially when I tried to talk about it, and asked my Mum about all that happened, it was awkward. She never went into much detail and although she never shut the conversation down, it would be changed reasonably quickly, and I could tell it held too much pain for her. She was just so hurt by the whole thing. In a way I felt for a long time it wasn't fair to ask anybody, Mammy or Daddy, because they were both so hurt over it. Hurt for what had happened to me, their baby, and by their own family's reactions and lack of support. It was too painful for them to talk about it. When I was younger, I took this as another hit to my own self esteem. I had caused everyone so much hurt and pain. My telling them what happened had caused such a big fall out. Just as Martin said it would. This whole thing seemed to be much more about the hurt and pain everyone else had gone through, than it was about my own need to access my past. This used to bug me a little, as it was my experience, my story, my life, my past. As a teenager I felt entitled to know and discuss what happened. I felt entitled to talk about it, especially as I was now in puberty and getting a better understanding of the world of sexuality and emotions. Yet I really felt, during these years, that I couldn't seem to talk to anyone about it. It was well into my adult years before I recognised and understood just how unseen I had really been, through the whole process. For years I saw the whole 'Martin thing', as being everyone else's story of pain. I avoided tending to my own feelings, in favour of not hurting other people's feelings. I avoided looking at the event because it caused so many problems for others. My looking at it or wanting to talk about it always seemed to be inconvenient - the wrong time - and although it was humoured as much as possible, I was generally told we could talk about it when I got older. So, once more I put it away and waited patiently for when I got older.

When I was in my late teens, I felt it was time to talk about it again. I needed to know more, and I was old enough now. My Mum gave me a letter of correspondence from Granny, from way back then. It discussed a little of what happened at the time. Granny was so angry in her letter, which for such a calm peaceful and loving Grandmother seemed out of character. I had never seen that side of her, and her tongue was sharp and bitter towards my Mum. The letter was cruel and unkind and essentially denied any truth to be accepted. It was written to my Mum, but it hurt me also. It hurt me for her, but also for me. I was so sad that I had caused such a big divide between them. I was close with my own Mum and couldn't imagine her not believing me, or turning her back on me, let alone speak to me this way. Once again, I felt alone, I felt awful for bringing it all up again. But I had nobody else I could talk to. I stopped asking my Mum, for a few years, and tried to ask my Dad...but he couldn't go there really and just got out of the conversation. It weighed heavily on my mind as a teen, and the less information I was given the more curious I was about the whole thing. I even remember asking my brothers if they remembered what had happened. I was so young it was hard to piece it all together, but I felt I needed to know in order to let it go. Everyone seemed awkward talking about it, but me. Yet it was my life, my memories, my story. This used to irritate me a little, as the pain in this story seemed to be all about everyone else, but what about me: the one who experienced it all? When do I get heard? I remember reading Granny's words in that letter, it may have been to Mam, but they were about me, and her lack of belief was not only denying Mammy, but she denied me in tandem.

Back when it all happened, when I told Mam and Dad what had happened and what Martin had done, my Dad was still a Policeman. Mam and Dad both decided that I should make an informal Statement to the Police if. The idea being in future, if I ever decided to press charges or in the event it happened to anybody else, I could testify it happened to me. It was to ensure I had some sort of back-up in the future if need be.

To this day I have no interest in using that Statement. This book I am writing is not as a means of damning anyone, but more as a means of voicing my experience in hopes that it may help others who have been silenced, or through similar events, to feel seen and not so alone. Perhaps even to help them come to some sort of understanding and means of moving on with their own lives. My experiences and feelings have been included as a means of giving perspective to the array of human interactions and psychology involved in such an event - with perspective and the ability to see from all sides - I feel it then becomes easier to dissolve the intense feelings of guilt, shame, embarrassment and confusion. I can see where my Parents were coming from in getting me to make a

Statement, especially with my Dad being a Policeman, as he had clearly seen it all before and knew what way the system worked.

I have a memory of this woman called Majella coming to the house. I knew she was a Policewoman and she was lovely. I have memory of sitting in my Dad's office, in what we called "The Den" (and what would later be my own bedroom), with Majella to have a chat. She asked me lots of questions. Then I remember saying goodbye to her and as she got into the car she handed me a teddy with an orange face and checkered blue and white shirt. I felt an incredible bond with her always, and still have that Teddy. For years after I held her in my mind as somebody who I grew a bond with.

The effects of what happened certainly played on my mind when it came to relationships. Through the years, for various reasons in my adult relationships, I ended up seeking therapy. I had had a series of issues, concerning sex, that led me to feeling I was broken and needed help. If I am to be completely honest: I felt so broken at times that I often struggled with a deep desire to not be here on many occasions and fought a darkness which would pull me under from time to time.

Although on the outside I was a reasonably contented person there was always an underlying default hatred and disgust of myself, which I fell into as soon as I felt I had acted wrong with another person. Using Hypnosis, I had hoped that maybe I could get rid of this. I had also hoped that maybe I could remember what happened as a kid. So, if that was causing any problems by itself, then I could consciously let it go and stop it from being a shadow in my life. I felt there were aspects of what had happened which affected me subconsciously and I needed to let them go. Consciously, I felt perhaps I was just broken as a person, and I would never be fixable. I even felt that perhaps none of it was to do with the abuse as a child at all, and perhaps I was just a broken person anyway. I hated on myself a lot and blamed myself for just being a defect of a human. I didn't like my personality. I didn't like much of my own self. I didn't even know my own self, and any little thing I felt I did wrong in life or regarding my interpersonal relationships, I hated on myself for. In Astrology: being a Virgo Sun with Scorpio Rising, deeply emotional, terribly analytical and somewhat of a perfectionist in some respects, it's not surprising I used these skills as a weapon on myself.

I carried awful guilt and shame for not being able to be the person I wanted to be. I saw myself as a crappy human, a waste of space, and emotionally too sensitive and too unstable. I saw myself as an irritation to others, and my own self. I hated being around myself quite a lot, and certainly hated even more the idea that if I felt like this, with me, then others surely felt like this with me too. I never fully accepted me for me. Therefore, when it came to having issues with sex and relationships, I once again took all the blame and assumed the issue was all me. I assumed it must have been to do with my actions, thoughts, emotions, body, insecurities and there were times I felt I was losing my grip on being here. I honestly, on many occasions, felt I was a waste of life. I felt if I wasn't able to navigate my emotions or other people's emotions well, and if I couldn't operate as a basic human and keep my life together, then I didn't deserve to be here. I felt that everything I did eventually ended up broken and it was my fault. I often didn't see the point in my being here; and fumbling around trying to make sense of life at times felt like a real mission. I always felt that my personality, emotions, and feelings were somehow just different to others. I thought that perhaps if I could just remember what happened fully, and see it wasn't as bad as I thought it was (just like everyone else said) then perhaps everyone else was right. Then I could just drop it. But my mind was on lockdown. It sounds like a contradiction, to want to remember it so I could let it go, but without the full memory I felt I would always be searching for the truth. Searching for what was wrong with me.

Searching for the truth began at an early age and was a theme I would see heavily feature throughout my life. Unearthing the reasons for why we do the things we do, why we are the way we are, why we are here, what our purpose and mission in life is, and how we can understand every situation from different perspectives in order to find peace and let go; I can now see how this was a skill I was honing at a very early age.

I was also afraid that if what was wrong with me was nothing to do with what happened as a kid, and I was just a broken person, that I was doomed forever...to a life where I hated myself for no reason, no cause. Without the full memory I would always have to rely on others, and so far, nobody was helping me. I needed to remember it for myself, my own truth, and then find my own way to release it all. You can't half let something go; you need to fully let it go. You can't half die, you need to fully die, in order to be reborn again.

In every therapy session it would take me right up to the moment, where I could see him, me, the room, the red light coming from the lamp on the side table, the games closet behind him, the open door, my nighty (nightdress), him, me, movement, flashes of what happened, then nothing. A void. A black dark empty space where my memories used to be. This always annoyed me. In my body I knew what happened and I knew I remembered it, as I had seen flashes of it through the years, but it was as though my mind would give me a glimpse and then shut down. I would see body parts, his face, my body, and glimpses of what happened. I could feel the emotions, fear and confusions, but it was as though they would flash into my mind but not long enough for me to see the picture. It always annoyed me that I was being denied access to my own memories! Surely it couldn't be so awful that they needed total erasure and censorship!

In my adult mind I had learned to come to terms with the idea that maybe it wasn't so bad. That's what anyone who knew about it would say, 'sure you were only kids'. Like that made it acceptable. I had come to adopt the same mind pattern they had: maybe it was nothing. Maybe I was making a big deal over nothing. I felt that's what everyone wanted, for me to feel it was nothing also...and I did; I began to accept that concept, yet my body felt differently around him. I would tell myself it was all just nothing, and maybe it was kids being kids; then as soon as he was in the room my body reacted, like a repelled magnet. I would feel a little weak and nauseous in my stomach and from nowhere would feel nervous, shy and almost pathetic and insecure. Disempowered and overpowered. I would go to a bathroom or find a way of being in a different place, because the energy just felt weird. I thought it must be my mind working overtime, and so I was hoping that in these therapy sessions I could just see it for what it was a let it go. Release it.

But it always seemed to come back to me. It was as though the more I told myself that it was nothing, the more my body reacted. The more I tried to ignore it, the more it would come up over and over again. It was as though a dirty secret which had been buried and was starting to smell. I was determined to unearth a truth which was now even hidden from myself. It was a secret again, and I didn't like that. Everyone else seems to think it's not a big deal, that even my thinking about it is simply making it more of a big deal than it was. So, I became silent, bobbing my head up for air and occasionally asking questions, then submerging once again to silence. Even in therapy my mind was telling me it wasn't any of my business.

Nothing I did ever really seemed to bring me any resolution. This mission to set myself free started in my teenage years and would continue well into my adult years.

***

CHAPTER EIGHT

FORGIVEN NOT FORGOTTEN

From a very young age, and all through the years, I have always been interested in the mind, psychology, self-development, self-discovery, the mind body and soul. I have always read various psychology and self-help books; spiritual books and I guess I have tried to be open minded with various concepts and ideas along the way. Trying on different ideas, to see what would sit with me, then letting them go as soon as they no longer served me. It has been a journey of trial and error, playing around with what resonates. My feelings of being broken through the years, on and off, led me on a mission in search of a better me. I was determined I wasn't broken and was sure I would find a way to come to terms with myself, who I was, and why I was the way I was. I was in search of something I had lost, myself. I was in search of Me; I just didn't realise it back then.

I was very lucky to grow up with parents who were so open minded and liked to discuss and ponder everything in life, spirituality and psychology. My Dad was a successful and incredible Hypnotherapist and Psychotherapist which allowed that curiosity to expand. Quite often, as an adult, myself, Mam and Dad, would talk about all manner of mind-bending ideas on humanity and our existence, into the wee hours of the morning. We were always fascinated by the human mind and behaviour. I found the world of the human psychology so fascinating, and I eventually studied some Hypnotherapy/ Psychotherapy myself, as well as many other alternative and complementary healing modalities.

In my late teen years, around the time I had begun asking more questions at home over what had happened as a kid, I remember first learning about the concept of forgiveness. The idea of forgiveness setting you free. It seemed if we were to truly feel forgiveness of the self and of others, it could transform one's life. So, I decided to try out this new belief system with regards to Martin, in hopes that I could fix the Me I didn't like, which was evident even back then.

'Forgiveness' I feel became this buzz word, which many spiritual teachers used. So, I decided to forgive Martin I so I could move on...so I didn't have to think about it anymore....so everyone else could forget about it and move on. When Martin and I were in the same room together, for me it always created such tension, and I clearly made others uncomfortable with my story. Granny also clearly wanted nothing but for the two of us to get on too. So, I decided the next time I saw him I would talk to him, which I hadn't done since I was 4 years old - over 13 years ago. I was going to be an adult and show him, and everyone else, that it was all over now. We could all move on and they could all be okay when we were in a room together. It also meant, if I could do this right, there was a promise of mental freedom for me. I could be free of thinking about it ever again, and it would never affect me, or so I thought! I just wanted to feel okay being in the same room together... and have everyone see me as a real adult who handled it all well! To take back control. In hindsight: I can see my naivety, lack of true understanding and development - as the outcome was not as expected. However, I can see that I was already on the road to self-confidence as the gutsy wee kid I was for doing that. How mature I was for doing my best to take charge of my own life.

I was about 16 or 17 years of age when I decided to try my new self-help tool out. We had a family gathering in Leitrim. Over the years there had been a number of these family gatherings. Martin would be there and I would inevitably hide myself out of the way, while he chilled and mingled with the family. My brothers, Joe and Pat, were always there for me on these occasions, they were so supportive. They never had to say or do much, but they always made me aware they were right behind me. They always made me aware they had my back, and without saying very much at all they would always find a really sweet and subtle way to let me know they knew the situation, and knew it made me uncomfortable. They would very sweetly find a way to put their hand on my back, while looking me in the eye and quietly, and softly, asking 'Are you okay?'. I'd nod gratefully and that would be it. That was all I needed. No show, no drama, just support. These situations always had me trading any feeling or emotions which would disempower me, for those of a mature adult, who nothing bothered. It was far safer for me to pretend I was okay, than to acknowledge how I was really feeling inside; nauseous and uncomfortable. To the outside world all was fine, but inside I just wanted to escape and run away, but I couldn't. I didn't want to make a scene or have any drama, I just wanted it to be over.

On this occasion, in Leitrim, it was a family party. We all went to the local nightclub in the town. My Mam and everyone knew I drank at this stage, and so did most other kids my age. So, it wasn't a big deal that I was drinking. I had a few for Dutch courage, then walked over to Martin who was standing alone at the edge of the dancefloor. All the aunties and uncles, cousins etc. were sat together chatting in a cubby area. As soon as they saw me move towards Martin I could sense their eyes on us, wondering what was going to happen. The same over the shoulder looks I was hoping this encounter would silence.

I said to him, 'Martin, we both know what happened. I want to move on forgive and forget about it all, can we do that?', his answer was 'I don't know what you're talking about', which blew me away. I knew that he knew, so I reminded him what I was talking about, and said 'You know what I'm talking about, when I was 4!'. He said: 'Sure we were only kids, it was nothing'. I wanted to vomit. I wanted to unleash my raging inner Tigers' claws and rip him apart for dismissing it just as everyone else had done. It was the first time this whole thing was out loud, out in the open, outside my head, and he belittled it with a twisted cold hard stare. He admitted it, which made it even more real to me. It wasn't hidden anymore. But his eyes were cool and empty. He pulled his top lip out over his bucked teeth, and sucked in his lower lip below them, as he looked away from me out over the dancefloor, as if I wasn't there, pretending I didn't exist. As if there was nothing more to say. We were done. His expression and body language left me cold. It had taken a lot of courage to do what I did, and I couldn't believe that not only did he acknowledge it but he belittled it like everyone else and shut me down, stood there ignoring me. After all that effort I felt worse about the whole thing. I learned, in that moment, that there was much more to this forgiveness tool than I had prepared myself for. I realised in that moment, that forgiveness meant much more, was much deeper and I hadn't forgiven him.

What's worse was, I once again had to pretend it was okay: I was all grown up now and did a really adult thing of confronting my demons. But confronting them just validated his acknowledgement that it happened, infuriated me that nobody believed it did happen and he had acknowledged the event but belittled it, and made it into nothing.

In the corner, in the cubby, everyone's antennas went up. They all hid it well and continued on whatever they were doing, but all with side glances and over the shoulder surveillance to see what would happen, would anything happen? I could feel the tension and I could feel their silent looks. Nothing happened. The night continued and I wrapped up the open wound again. I had retracted my forgiveness, now I was angry with him, for his admission and dismissal.

As time went on I got used to once again putting my feelings away. This was a familiar skill which I had begun to master at a young age. The skill involved pretending the past never happened, in order to make others feel more comfortable, which in turn made me feel more comfortable with them but not with myself. Everyone could 'get on' with it again, even Martin.

I found every time I tried out my 'forgiveness' on the whole Martin situation, within myself, to allow myself move on with it all, something came along to test me on this. I guess it's the Universe's way of saying 'Okay, so you think you have it this time. Let's try it out. Here's a test to see whether you really have forgiven!'.

What I have learned so far, is that forgiveness does not mean you must give up part of who you are and forget what happened, nor does it excuse what happened as being right or wrong, but it allows you to look at the overall picture with kindness and compassion, with perspective. Neither is forgiveness a one-time fix all solution, for there were so many facets to this experience. Therefore, time will always throw a new curveball, a new experience which calls for forgiveness in a new way once more, in another way for myself and all those involved. For me, through the years, I realised that it wasn't only Martin I needed to forgive. But it was also Myself, and those who I felt unseen by, those who I felt at the time took sides or pretended it didn't happen. Those who I felt never believed me. I had learned to try and understand why people reacted how they did, this helped me to forgive. I had come to this new understanding of 'they didn't know how to cope with the whole thing'. Seeing their confusion and possible pain, helped me to forgive also. Then as years progressed, people carried on doing what had always worked for them and so nothing ever changed, and I kept learning new ways to forgive over and over in silence. There was still so much old pain and trapped emotions that needed to be released. But being human is imperfectly perfect, and all about growth.

I also felt I carried the burden and had to forgive my Mam and Dad's pain, and the hurt they experienced over the lack of support they received. I had to forgive myself for causing such friction, divide and pain in our family. I had to forgive myself for the shame and guilt which I had put on myself. Forgiveness was a weed with much bigger, and deeper roots than I could have understood in those early years. It's taken me a lot of time, and I'm not sure to what extent I will ever fully be able to release into forgiveness, but it seems like a constant process which I am getting much better at it.

I find when I am not emotionally connected to the memories; when not in Martin's company, or not forced to listen to stories about him; when I can see the trauma and difficulties he had experienced in his own past, where I feel compassion for his own childhood, or see him as just another human, I feel I can be a little more understanding. Having studied some Psychology, I also understand the effects his own traumas may have had on him. These may have caused him to act out in ways he may not have fully understood at the time, himself. I can understand that I was an easy target as I was only in Leitrim once a year. There is a safe distance in that. However, when we are around each other, sharing the same energetic space, it is as though old records and old thought patterns kick in to play, as a protective measure. It is a little more difficult to navigate those feelings of forgiveness. It's as though my physical reactions override my mental capacity to control my feelings. Luckily it doesn't happen very often, but it takes practice.

Interestingly, in more recent years I have come to realise there is a thick thread which I have found hard to sever, with regards to forgiveness. I have realised that every time I allow myself to move on from Martin and what happened, I am pulled back by a double edge sword. All I ever wanted was to feel seen, acknowledged for my truth, and not hide it anymore. To not have to pretend for others it didn't happen. To not have to pretend for others, so they can feel okay. To not have to pretend I'm okay, so I am accepted and not rejected. To not be made feel as though it never happened, as though I, or my Mam, lied. This has been what has hurt the most. All I wanted was the same respect, support and acknowledgement that Martin got. In many ways I feel there was never a fair trial with us. It felt as though everyone stood by him and took his side while I was silenced just because I was a child, just because I lived further away. I was too young to speak up for myself, and the years from then to now meant I had to find my own voice in the silence. Therefore, for me to truly let go and forgive, it means I must accept that my story will always fall back into their silence. Silence which always left me standing in the shadow. To let go, I must first accept that I may never be seen.

I have a belief that before we come to this world, we get to choose our life experiences. All life experiences, both good and bad, are what shapes us as humans. In fact, I have come to the understanding that good and bad are born from the same place. That perhaps they are in fact simply tools for our awakening. They are simply signposts toward finding ourselves, which inevitably leads us back to source or God or Home, whatever you want to call it. It is these experiences and life lessons, which ultimately makes us stronger as humans and I also believe, in many ways, that these lessons we go through in life, are a means of releasing past trauma or inherited suffering of our ancestors.

When I began to learn Astrology and could see how certain wounds and challenges were already written in our birth charts, it somehow made all these experiences more bearable. As an Holistic Therapist who uses Astrology and is reading charts for people all the time, I can see how we come here to have a specific set of experiences. I have had many clients who have experienced early childhood trauma, which has been visible in their personal charts. When my clients see that the experience was not their fault, and in some way simply a part of their journey, unique to them, its truly incredible the healing can come from this. When we can uncover more of who we truly are, reconnect with our wisdom and learn to interpret our world and experiences, I feel this is where true healing happens.

I also feel, in many ways, history repeats itself. Perhaps what happened as a kid for me, has happened for many of my ancestors before. Perhaps they were not able to release the pain and didn't have the knowledge we have today, and with my letting go this energy never has to repeat itself.

Before awakening to the higher wisdom of my experiences there was some unfolding to do. When I began to do the work on myself, one thing I realised was how I had learned my inner world and outer world did not align. From an early age I learned that following my instinct, inner voice, led me to fall-out and ultimately: rejection. I discovered that my actions in some way made people dislike me and I began to feel safer living my life based on how I felt people saw, and accepted me, versus being true and authentic to myself. I did this for so many years, that it became automated. I was a people pleaser and somebody who seemingly just went with the flow. It was easier to follow the herd than to have my own voice. Keeping the peace and not standing out was much safer. My inner voice was no longer to be trusted; it got me into trouble. Although I became adept at judging the energy of a room, or people, very quickly I found when it came to knowing the difference between what instinct was and what was an old fear playing as a record, it became impossible to know the difference. Therefore, rather than be wrong I judged my external environment, and sought my answers there instead of inside, and lived my life according to what seemed acceptable to my outside world. I lost the connection to my inner knowing, when it came to people and relationships, and it would be many years before I would realise just how disconnected I had become to my own self.

It would take some major life events and some Hollywood style drama to finally shake me awake and begin to see how lost I truly was. Now, I had begun my journey from losing my Self to searching for my Self. Only time would tell whether I could ever truly set myself free.

***

PREVIEW CHAPTERS – PART II

Coming Home

To Me

A Journey of Getting Lost
and Coming Home to Me

Part II: Searching for My Self

CHAPTER ONE

GUT INSTINCTS & BODY REACTIONS

It's funny how your life can completely change, literally in the blink of an eye. One moment you are engaged to be married and getting ready to send out the wedding invitations; the next you are waiting patiently for traffic to let you turn out of a hotel carpark where you have just spent a lovely Halloween weekend together, when you notice a curious pop-up on your Fiancé's phone!

It's truly amazing how, in life, we take these small moments for granted. When we are stuck on a motorway behind a car that's driving really slowly: how many stop to wonder 'Perhaps my being slowed down is to stop me from getting into an accident further ahead'? When we are running late for a plane, how many stop to think: 'Perhaps I wasn't meant to fly because I would be missing a valuable opportunity if I stay'?.

On this occasion I was sitting in the Archway of the Carlow Hotel, waiting for a string of traffic queuing up at the lights to go over the bridge, waiting for somebody to let me out onto the road. On many other occasions I could have been furious and cursing the traffic, cursing those who were rude and unkind not to let me out onto the road. On other occasions I may have felt victimised and taken it personally that nobody could 'see' me or notice me. On this occasion however I found a gap or space in the matrix, which quite literally changed my life for good. Sometimes 'waiting' is offering you a moment to become aware, present, in the 'now'.

As we sat in the car, queuing to get out onto the main road, Tom decided he needed to charge his phone, so he plugged it into the glovebox in my car. There was a USB port in there which allowed you to hook up a phone to it and charge. Tom opened the glove box, reached in and pulled out the charger cable. He attached it to his phone and the screen came to life highlighting he was now on low battery, which was charging, and connected live to power from the car. He had an old Samsung phone with an App he had installed on it for cleaning files and stopping it from running slow. I know this because I had discovered and installed this great same App on my phone. This App caused the phone to have 'pop-up' advertisement displayed on the charge screen, as a kind of Banner Advert.

Now, having worked with marketing and advertising at the time, I knew how these adverts worked. They essentially track things you have searched or interacted with online or on your social media. They then bring up the same or similar pages you have visited, by means of pop-up adverts, ways of getting you back to that page or to get you to interact with similar pages or by means of selling you something that you may be interested in, based on your search and internet usage.

Because I had the same App on my phone, I knew that it would only display pop-ups relating to things I had already interacted with, and the pop-up I saw on Tom's phone that morning was not what I expected at all.

I would like to say, that as I write this to you right now, my heart has suddenly started pounding: I can feel the artery in my neck swell, I feel hot, my chest feels tight and I've noticed I'm taking lots of long deep de-stressing sighs and breaths. Isn't it incredible what a simple passing memory can do? Although I am being present with this emotion and allowing it to come and pass, I know the intensity of what it symbolises. The intensity of the shadows which grew from that time. It's as though my body knows what comes next. It's as though I am at the top of the crest of a rollercoaster and panicking in myself because there's nowhere left to go but down, steeply, quickly, and with an adrenalin rush that may be the only thing that ensures my heart stays pumping to keep me alive! I would also like to add, as I sit here writing, that I am doing everything in my power not to write the next part. Again, it's like my ego, mind and body are all stopping me from having to relive the incredible stress of it all again. It's as though my body mind and soul know that I barely made it out alive the first time, and they are not sure they want to go there again. They are not sure they can survive that a second time. My body is literally shivering and shaking now, as though it were cold... but I am not at all cold. It is a kind of body shock, yet I feel completely present and aware of all the changes. These thoughts and moments of complete awareness give me comfort and remind me of how far I have come. These moments of awareness, as though I were watching my mind and body react, bring me comfort in the knowing that I have spring-boarded past who I was, into a more humbled and authentic me. Yet, I know I am digressing also... see... I had to catch myself again! The real-time example of how meditative thought works! You simply catch yourself in the distraction and come back to centre.

I find it easier to sit here writing about how I am feeling, trembling, rather than to go to the next part of the story. But I know

I must. I stop myself and remind myself that it's time. It's time to write this and just get it all out. It's time to share the story in hopes that others who have been through the same might feel some comfort or relief. It's time to just get it out from the shadows and into the light. I remember when all this happened, I swore if I survived the craziness of that time, I would do my best to ensure other women who are going through the same, would not feel as alone and isolated as me. This is my tribute and support to them.

As I write, my friend who I met while travelling in Colombia, messaged me. Her messaging reminds me had it not been for the next part of this story – of which I am doing a great job of avoiding – I wouldn't have had so many adventures thereafter. From the ashes rises the phoenix, but I guess it's time to sift through the ashes once again and get on with it! Jesus! This is not as easy as it sounds! For those contemplating writing a book, my advice is keeping banging that door down and one day you'll get through – As I write this I even wonder will I make it through myself or will this end up another saved 'Word' Doc on my computer. It's beautiful to think that someday, these words may transform from disjointed paragraphs to a book??

On I go…

The pop up on his phone had a cartoon type graphic with a speech bubble coming out of its mouth saying *'Hi – Are you single?'*, I knew it was an advert so initially I just passed no great attention to it. I was busy anyway, trying to find a car to let me out across the road so we could get on the road back to Dublin. We had a long drive ahead. But I couldn't get the image out of my mind. The image of it would flash before my eyes. I would feel nauseous with sudden cold sweaty butterflies in my tummy. Then I would let it go, in favour of my being over-reactive and coming across dramatic. I didn't want to be one of *those* girlfriends who over-reacts, is jealous or who doesn't trust her boyfriend – 'Uch, no way I didn't want to be one of *THOSE* stereotypes', I thought.

This really bugs me now, because in hindsight I can completely see how the movies, TV, media, advertising, marketing, and all the brainwashing and programming we have received from birth has manipulated and distorted our understanding of both ourselves, and each other. Our external world is like one big advertisement. Telling us who we are, what to wear, drink, eat, smell like, how to exercise and how to be as a human. TV and Movies have taught us false perceptions over who we are, who others are. We have lost contact with ourselves. In hindsight I can now see how my being afraid to be seen as one of *THOSE* stereotypes, came from narratives we are fed. Narratives which are there to 'Hush' women from connecting in with their natural sense, their natural instincts. Media and TV and Movies have designed such stereotypes as a means of supressing your judgement down to self-criticism. What I didn't know then, but I do know now...there is always a reason you are thinking the things you are thinking, and when they come from the gut and not the head, then you should pay attention and ask yourself why?

Back then I shook it off and thought to myself, 'There's no way Tom is on a dating App, or looking elsewhere, or cheating! Right?' He had only proposed to me a year ago and we were about to send out our wedding invitations. Anyway, he was a good guy. He was the kind of guy who helped Old Grannies across the street. He volunteered with disadvantage people and youth. He had worked with disabilities. He was a sportsman and a gentleman. There was no way he was double-crossing me? Right?'.

Quite literally I remember shaking my head, like a Magic-8 ball, looking for an alternative different answer to the one which was showing up in my head. I shook my head to get rid of the thought. Then focused on the traffic again. 'Damn traffic, why won't anybody let me out?' I thought. Then the image came to my mind once again, then the thoughts I just had all came back; again, I shook them away. I was being bombarded by these re-occurring thoughts, which seemed to get louder and more persistent every time I shook them away and returned to waiting on the traffic to let me out. Now I felt my frustration rise with this bloody line of traffic, 'Why can't anyone see me?', I thought! Why doesn't anyone have the bloody manners to let me out?', but the *out* I was in desperation for was not from the traffic, it was from my own mind! Christ, the torment!

Finally, the traffic moved and a car stopped to let me through, out and onto the opposite side of the road. We were heading home now, and I could forget all about it. I could avoid being that doubting girlfriend who is paranoid and delusional! There was no way was I right and I would embarrass myself by simply bringing it up with him! I was only meters up the road and there they were again in my head: the pestering images on his phone: the 'What if your wrong?...and... 'What if you don't say a word?...the pestering feeling I needed to do something, the gut reaction... the horrendous retching gut reaction! I had to say something! But I didn't want to! But there was something else inside me driving me now and I almost felt powerless to what came next!

I decided right there and then that we needed to talk. When I say right there and then I mean it. Once I decided to let it out and confront it, once the adrenalin filled my body with enough power to rip down the walls that were holding me together, there was no stopping me. The next gap, clearing or space that I saw I was turning the car in and there it was, an empty abandoned carpark. The gaps in the concrete growing with weeds. The depressing grey of the concrete slabs echoes of what was to come.

I suddenly indicated left and pulled into the open courtyard, in what was only slightly short of a handbrake turn. I turned off the car and turned sideways in my seat to face a completely unknowing, and somewhat slightly bewildered looking Tom. Then in a tone that neither he or I had ever witnessed coming from my mouth, I said 'You need to tell me what the F*** is going on! I want to know everything. I want to know what the F*** is going on? Who are you seeing and what dating website are you on!'? I demanded to know all the social media platforms he was on also. I said 'Tell me it all and don't make me pull it from you, because I will. Now is your chance to come clean and tell me what the F*** you're doing and not to leave anything out, because I will find out!'

WOW! Even just writing that now makes me shake! I was so bloody strong there! At the time I had NO idea where those words came from, I had no idea how I managed to phrase them so well, I had no idea I was capable of such conviction and MAN, did I sound convincing! Especially when only moments before I was so doubtful of those thoughts. It's like there was a huge surge of sturdy strength and conviction which came from a deeper level of myself, a level I had never before tapped into. I remember at the time feeling a sense of letting go into myself, like if I went with the flow of whatever came though me it would come out right. I remember just after I spoke, the silence was vast and I clearly remember feeling like the words I had just delivered were not the surface me, but whatever was coming through me. I felt almost possessed for a moment, not by any radical disconnection to my being, but in a way that was not at that time familiar to me. I was possessed with a strength. It would be this incredible strength which would guide me through the hurricane to my survival. It would be this connection to my inner voice, which I had abandoned and lost for so many years, which led me to handling this whole thing like a boss, and surviving how I did! Lessons I would in time see more clearly.

***

CHAPTER TWO

LIFE CAN CHANGE IN THE BLINK OF AN EYE

He didn't move and just faced forward in his seat. He was eerily cool, calm and unphased. I found this a little odd and unsettling, considering my intense delivery only moments before. He didn't at all seem surprised by my words and it was as though nothing had even happened. His coolness left me a little cool also. His lack of emotion to such an accusation and outburst would surely evoke some sort of emotion! I repeated part of my speech in hopes to jog his memory and perhaps bring him along in the moment with me, to catch him up a little! He asked me what I was talking about, as though I was mad; that's what people do when they want you to think you are crazy! They put it back on you, and make you think you are overreacting. But I persisted, I was too committed now, 'What's on your phone Tom? I saw the pop-ups and know how they work. What dating site are you on? I work in marketing and know they follow you around. So, I know there's something going on!', He became weirdly victimised and accused, as if from nowhere – a sudden click into gear of emotions. He denied it over and over and I remember wondering; if he's denying it so much why would he not offer me to look at his phone - wouldn't that be the logical conclusion to this, if there was nothing to hide? I remember thinking this and not saying it.

I was still in 'I don't want to be that stereotypical girlfriend who needs proof' mode; or that stereotypical girlfriend whose boyfriend now needs to surrender his privacy for her paranoia, and that's a difficult road to come back from.

I've never been the kind of person to snoop behind somebody else's back, to look in their phone or laptop like you see them doing on TV. I would hate for my own privacy to be intruded on, so I certainly wouldn't do it to somebody else ... or at least never up until then! However, on this occasion I needed for him to prove to me that I was imagining things. To prove to me that what I saw was not what I thought it was. I wanted him to offer me, and not for me to ask him. Then his body pushed forward toward the glovebox, where his phone was. He took it out, looked at it limply in his hand (in a 'whatever', kind of fashion). He assured me there was nothing on it. He didn't turn it on or do anything with it but just held it as a dull and useless visual aid in his hand; then returned it back to the glove box as quickly as he had taken it out, saying there was nothing on his phone. We continued this for a few moments until I saw him move his body forward again. As though he was going to take the phone out again, but he didn't. He stopped himself. I thought this weird. I was so present with myself at this moment that it was hard not to see that. Then I called him on it: saying 'So why won't you show me your phone then? Why did you take it out, but not turn it on or show it to me?'. He gave some ridiculous excuse that began to lead me to believe there was something more to all of this.

I then confronted him and said I saw something on his pop up about sex or dating or something? I said I know how this works and I know that these banner ads follow you around from sites you have been on. I told him I wanted to know what he was doing! He said: 'It was probably porn' - in a really passive casual way, as if we had had this conversation before – which we hadn't ever. I asked him to show me. I wanted to see. Actually... I demanded... to see the porn sites he was on and I wanted to see what he was looking up. If it was so casual and 'whatever' then surely, he would show me to prove it!

It was in these next few moments, I have absolutely no idea why, but a source within me began asking questions which were so perfect, they seemed to draw from him the answers I needed to hear.

I was asking questions, worded so perfectly that he had nowhere to hide in them. They demanded an honest answer. It was insane the answers I was getting and even more impressive the questions I was asking, or how I knew how to ask. I was asking questions that were completely unrehearsed. They came from a mindset which had never been in my sphere of thought before. It was like I was feeling the moment, opening my mouth, questions came out that even I was shocked I was asking. Even in that moment I was wondering where they came from and why I was asking them! Especially why was I asking Tom, the man I loved, the man I was supposed to be engaged to and marrying! Questions which seemed to come from the darkness into the light, from a place of nothingness to a place of being. It was happening in real time and because I was so incredibly present with myself, I felt as though I was a witness to my own unfolding. As soon as I would speak, I would think 'Where the hell did that come from? How did I know to ask that question?'. So, I did as any good saleswoman would do…. I did very little talking and let him fill the empty and awkward silences…

He began to open his phone, in a very weak and fumbling manner. Like how you would see an elderly person fumble and swipe on a phone to get it to work; slow, weak, with a kind of feeble and unsure effort. But he did it as though it was normal. His air was unshaken, cool and normal. His answers were equally cool and unshaken, as though he was ordering steak from a menu. He weakly and calmly, slowly, opened his phone and opened the internet. Like reeaaalllll slow! My eyes were like a hawk to see could I spot anything he was likely to swipe away or get rid of before I could have a chance to see. I was waiting to catch a glimpse of an opened window in his browser, a text on his phone, something or anything which would trap him, which would help me realise I wasn't crazy! I had sharp focus and heightened awareness of everything and every move now. But he didn't falter and almost seemed as though he was purposely slow, in a way that said he had nothing to hide and was happy to prove it. It was as though his slowness was to make him look extra calm.

I asked him to show me the kind of porn sites he was on, and he clicked into the site. This felt strange; I don't recall having had any porn chats with him before. I mean, I assume most or all guys watch porn but I guess it wasn't something I ever confronted or wanted to know about.

I asked him to show me what he would normally look up. Even this clever guidance was beyond me, and I was impressed with myself as this was happening – how the hell did I know to ask him to show me rather than tell me, or not allow myself to jump to conclusions? He showed me some of the sites and pages he looked up and I probed him asking 'And what else?'; he would answer and I would say 'And what else?'; he would show me more and I would repeat my probing, 'And what else?'. Over and over, until he had nothing more to show and then I demanded 'What else?!', as I knew there was something, he wasn't telling me. He would say there was nothing more and I would keep questioning him. Every time I pushed there seemed to be more. I had, in 15minutes become an expert interrogator.

I probed again, not satisfied. Then he admitted that he would go on to 'LiveCams' - as if I was supposed to know what that meant. I had no idea what that was. He said that the site he goes onto is 'IM Live' and he usually goes into this thing called 'Room of games'. This stuck in my head because he said these same words over and over, on a few occasions throughout the chat. I didn't catch it at the time, but it's incredible how my mind was able to bring it to awareness at a later stage when I was more relaxed. He had repeated it several times, it seemed to be important to him, almost like he shouldn't say it but had to repeat it so I would know. It was weird.

Still to this day that word makes me feel nauseous - 'LiveCams'. It makes me feel ill because it symbolises all that it represented and all that was to come from that moment thereafter. That word represented my world crashing; it represented my discovery of a life which I was not part of, and which was completely hidden from me. It represented a person who I didn't know and represented a secret personality he had hidden from me. It represented my inability to see or know about any of this and it represented how blind I was, how disconnected I was from my own self.

I had no idea what this 'LiveCams' was, and I asked him to explain it. He said that: 'You just go onto this website to look at these people. They are in rooms siting there, not doing a whole lot, but you can interact with them if you have an account and pay'.

This seemed really messed up to me! It was a kind of Red-Light District of the internet. It sounded, to me, like women who had been made into sex slaves and who were being prostituted for men's titilation and abuse online. It sounded pretty seedy and messed up to me. But I couldn't let him see any judgement. I couldn't let him see my reaction. If I was to react, it would shut him down. If he felt unsafe or judged, there was no way he would tell me more. So, I learned to be still, silent and unjudgmental, trying to understand what the hell was going on here.

He said he hadn't had an account and had not done anything on there since before we were together, which seemed like proper bullcrap to me... why would he go onto these 'Rooms' and just watch, and not participate? I'm not sure which is worse: the idea of him interacting with these women behind a computer screen like a dirty old man or him just watching, like some sort of weird perverted and secretive peeping tom! He explained that these LiveCams were live cameras of women in a room, who you could see masturbating and doing all sorts of sex acts. You could ask them to do things and you would pay them. I asked him did he have to pay for this and he said no. I asked over and over and he said that he didn't pay for them. I knew he was lying for some reason; after all here was a man I thought I knew everything about, and now I am seeing he's watching porn several times a day and watching women live in these LiveCam rooms. I knew I needed to be suspicious of everything.

Knowing Tom admitted to watching porn, I asked him how frequent it was? For some unknown reason I felt this was important, or rather 'The Flow' that was coming through me felt it was important for me to ask. I also wanted to keep an open mind, knowing guys watch porn, but assuming it's not all the time or some sort of unhealthy obsession – because that would be a problem! I wanted to be open and okay with him watching it, so he felt safe and knew that I would be okay with it. So, he didn't have to hide that part of him from me anymore. So, I could be a 'cool' girlfriend who was caring and understanding. So I could be 'cool' unlike other 'stereotypical' girls on TV who would freak out! I felt whatever was to come from this chat, if I could find a way to understand him, perhaps I could then accept it and we could go back to being in that good place we were in – being engaged, happy and on cloud nine.

I remained opened, as he answered. He told me that he watched porn... wait for it.... A few times.... not a month, not a week, A DAY! Then followed this up with, what he must have felt was a softening blow, by saying 'Sometimes I only click in to see the picture and then click out straight away. Sometimes I don't even go into it to watch a video... I'll click in and out!'

Can I just say at this moment I was like...? What the actual f**k!? The first blow was bad enough to know that he watches with such incredible frequency, which said to me that sex is on his mind all the time, all day... I was trying to figure out when the heck did he have time to watch so much of it, or even to check in an out of it! That absolutely blew me away! I imagined him in work, working with clients and with work colleagues, suddenly getting aroused, as if from nowhere, and running to the bathroom. I imagined him taking a crap and watching porn. Having a pee and watching porn. Getting frustrated in work and excusing himself to go to the bathroom to watch porn. Then I began to see him at the home we shared; in my memory wondering all those times he went to the bathroom, was it to watch porn... to just click in and out?! My paranoia ate at me like a cancer, it ate at me like a virus seeping through my veins. I felt so deceived and concerned over the secrecy and frequency.

Then he followed up repeating himself again, saying that sometimes he doesn't even look, he just clicks in and out of it.... that's nearly worse, I thought! Why, why would you need to click in and then out? I remember asking him this…. wondering why he would even bother to just click in and out, what purpose did that serve? My understanding up to that point was that porn was a means to an end. Guys clicked in, watched what they watched, jerked off and clicked out…. job done! I was really confused then as to why he would click in, for the purposes of sorting himself out, but then not do anything… leaving himself high and dry (if ever that saying had a place to be used, it was here – don't you think?!). This made no sense. What kind of satisfaction would somebody get from that? What need did that satisfy and what the hell does that mean then?... that he's constantly aroused all day?... clicking in to be a voyeur and clicking out? …full of testosterone for the day? He said that we would let himself build up and then do it when he was ready. What does that even mean, and why? I told him this concerned me.

It suddenly made so much sense to me, and as if from nowhere I began to have flashbacks of so many times where I would see him go to the bathroom with his phone. Sometimes he would be gone for a long time and would make jokes over having 'a good dump' when he finally emerged some-time later. I had flashbacks of my 'feelings' of insecurity at those times, my shoving them all away, telling myself I'm just being insecure. I'd think to myself I'm being paranoid over how long he has been in the bathroom. I didn't know I knew, but somehow it had crossed my mind before, but I shoved my paranoia away. How did I know and not realise I knew? How was I having, what seemed like random stray paranoid thoughts, and not think they were somehow relevant!? I can now recall often feeling there was something I was missing, or that some of these trips to the bathroom didn't feel quite right to me. I remember questioning them in my mind, but at a very subtle level where these feelings were dismissed as soon as they arose. Still to this day, I feel a little queasy at this, more because of how accurate I was and yet didn't know it. I feel nauseous that I missed it. I feel nauseous of the frequency and how well he hid it and how I never saw it. I feel nauseous that this existed, and I felt that I was partly to blame.

When he admitted to the frequency and that he checked in and out simply to just look at the girls there, I remained still and calm. Un-judgemental as possible. I needed him to feel safe to speak with me; I needed him to feel safe to confess to me; I felt there was more, and I needed to get all the information I could from him. If I had learned anything from all the self-development and study through the years, I learned that people will only close down if they themselves feel threatened or attacked or judged. If they feel safe, understood and have the opportunity to do so - to unburden themselves - most people will choose the safe option. I knew I needed to remain calm and open to him. Then BAM... another blow!

I asked him: with regards to the LiveCam's did he ever pay for sex? He said no. He said he had an account with them years before he met me, which he closed down. He said that you can just go into the LiveCams and look around and not do anything. He showed me the websites that he used but didn't say anything more. I asked him was he still spending money and did he still have an account? He denied having done anything else in there and denied spending money since we have been together.

I told him I wanted to know what else he had been doing and why I saw a dating app pop-up on his phone? I asked him straight out whether he had been seeing somebody else behind my back? He said no. I asked again. He said no. I said I didn't believe him and then there it was.... he blurted out and admitted he had been in contact with somebody he met on a dating website.

This was the same dating website/app where we had met over five years ago...the one which led us to getting engaged and planning our wedding, which was due next August.... only 10 months from then. The same wedding, we had just finalised and were about to send invitations out for that Christmas. The same wedding which now seemed pretty questionable... how the hell are you supposed to cancel a wedding?

I remember having nightmares as a teen and young adult about getting married and having to cancel it.... having to tell my parents, the guests and my future husband that I wasn't able to get married... being at the wedding itself knowing I made a terrible mistake and running away from the day. I swear, I actually had that nightmare a few times as a kid. Who could know that someday it might actually be a reality... and here I was, about to marry a man who I no longer even recognised! This seems dramatic now... but just you wait and see what was to come!

He continued with his confession. He said that he had been messaging a girl called 'Leticia V' who he met on the dating site before we got together. My face held its composure, whilst it drained of colour, whilst hair stood up on my neck and across my body like a wave, and whilst a flush of cold sweat ran across my still and unemotive body. I was holding my self together, remaining as calm as I could... while some other woman's name crawled down my back like nails down a chalkboard!

He said that there was nothing in their friendship and it was simply just friendship. He said they met up a few times, maybe 3-4 times, over the past 5 years for coffee.

Silence....

My brain yelled at him in frustration, while my face appeared calm... '5 F****** Years???!!' I yelled in the silence of my mind! We had been going out well over 5 years and I knew, and had met most if not all, of his friends and girlfriends.... or I certainly knew who was who at this stage. So, who the hell was this new name? Why did I not know about her?! Why had he never mentioned her?! Who the hell is this man I am supposed to marry...? Could he be keeping a whole other life from me? Surely not!? I knew all of his past girlfriends, we had chatted about all our past relationships, to the point that he himself even admitted he had a very limited past of both dating and relationships?!

***

ACKNOWLEDEGMENTS

My heartfelt thanks to all the beautiful Souls who have walked with me on this crazy but magical journey we call life. To all those who have welcomed me into their hearts just as I am. To all those who have supported me in my stepping into a more authentic and intuitive version of myself. To all those who took a chance on me, believed in me, and were there for me when I needed you the most – I am forever in gratitude.

To my Mother: in more ways than one, I would not be here had it not been for you. You have quite literally allowed me to open and bloom like a flower. You have been the light and beacon in every storm. For you I will never have enough words, or books of words, to convey my never-ending love, appreciation, depth of gratitude, and bond with you. 'I don't know if you know, but when we miss each other so, Look up... I'll meet you at the moon' (Imelda May) XXX

To my Father: Thank you for being You! For showing me what it means to be a Healer, a daughter, and a friend. You always believed in me, listened to me, and saw the strength and will in me before I ever knew it myself. You always encouraged me to follow my heart, not to worry about what others think and you taught me so much of the healing gifts I have today. Whenever my heart broke or I lost myself, you were always there for me; allowing me to make mistakes and encouraging me to be my person in the world. Even after death, your guiding hand helped me turn some of the most challenging moments of my life into gold. I miss you so much and I Love you XXXX.

To my Brothers: Thank you both for your love, support and always listening to me saying 'Do you remember when we were kids ...' As an incredibly nostalgic creature, I can say I had such a wonderful childhood with you both. I often miss the simple days. No words can express how much I love you both. Thank you for your imprints XX.

To Anna: with your kindness, compassion, wisdom, and generosity you opened the door and gave me the opportunities to heal myself in ways I could never have imagined possible. Your healing gifts and incredible depth of heart offered me the strength and support to embrace my own healing talents. Your belief in me and encouragement to step into my power, when I was unable to do it for myself, I can never have enough words to thank you with.

For YOU, I am truly grateful XX.

To Damien: my beautiful friend. Your strength, support, courage, wisdom, and boundless tenacity have influenced so much of both who I am as a person, and as an entrepreneur. Though you are no longer with us, I can often feel your energy. I know you are looking over my shoulder, giving me the strength to believe in myself, like you have always done. You saw in me what I could not see in myself, and you have been such an integral part of my journey. You were the rock and life raft in some of my darkest moments. I miss you terribly XX.

To my Dearest Friend Erica: I feel truly blessed to have you in my life. I always feel the fullest expression of who I am is nurtured, supported, and in bloom, in your presence. Although we are oceans apart, I feel constantly inspired by your love. You are a truly beautiful soul as a Mother, a wife, an entrepreneur, a Healer, a creative, and most of all, a friend.

Thank you to Lizzy Shortall who I began this journey, as a writing buddy. Having accountability for each other as we birthed our first books together, was a beautiful experience.

Thank you also to my Beta Readers who gave such amazing feedback on my books. I am glad it was a rollercoaster you enjoyed. To those who gave me huge confidence in knowing I was doing the right thing by releasing this into the world. I am so grateful my words have already begun to help so many, even before it was published. Thank you, Maryam Nawaz, on Fiverr from Pakistan, who was an incredible help in formatting my books and taking the stress out of getting my books up and online. To Lisa Jane of Butterfly Creation, for helping me format my book covers to get them online. To Carrie Green, the FEA, and all my friends and connections in the Online Business world, as well as my Astrology, Reiki, and Herbal friends; all of who have been an incredible source of support through this process.

Thank you to all my Teachers, Mentors, the Elders of our communities, my Ancestors whose torch I bear and whose wisdom I endeavour to pass on as best I can, while walking this road. Thank you to my Guides, and those who are both seen and unseen, who are forever in my heart. What an opportunity to be born in these times.

***

ABOUT THE AUTHOR

Deborah J. Kelly was born a country girl in the rural South East of Ireland. She now lives in the suburbs of Dublin. She is a Holistic Therapist, Speaker, Reiki Teacher, Astrologer, Mentor, Podcast Creator, Artist, Entrepreneur, and Writer.

As a child, she was creative, quiet, and a curious wee thing. She loved spending time in nature whether watching activities in the grass beneath her feet, playing in the trees, splashing in ponds, picking blackberries, making mud pies, or watching the stars above in the night sky. Fascinated by nature and the human experience, even as a small girl, she would ask herself 'What is it all about?'

She loved to write poetry and journal. She enjoyed writing short stories and creating cartoons and comics. She loved to record and play DJ on her radio, something she would later turn her skills to as a Podcast host and creator of 'The Intrepid Wisdom Podcast' (www.intrepidwisdom.com available on Spotify & iTunes). Deborah also loved to sketch and draw. She was always participating in whatever local art competitions were available. Nicknamed by her primary school teacher as 'The Doodler' she had more art supplies and sketch pads than an art and hobby shop. Upon leaving school she attended NCAD (National College of Art & Design). She worked full time as a Care Assistant to people with severe disabilities. She later returned to studying, specialising in Interior Design and Interior Architecture. After this, she worked in small start-up and medium-sized furniture and design companies. Here she worked in sales, design, admin, office manager, marketing and advertising, accounts, etc. Due to her experience in these businesses, she learned the ins and outs of entrepreneurism and of running a company. This was something that she would later apply while setting up her own Holistic business.

Through the years Deborah has travelled around the world and studied many subjects at home and abroad, from Hypnotherapy/ Psychotherapy to Reiki, Reflexology, Astrology, Meditation, Herbal Medicine, Mayan Cosmology, Acupressure and so much more. She has, and still, collects wisdom from around the world as a means of sharing these practical tools with others.

Little would she know it at the time, but she was always on a quest for truth, wisdom, and understanding. This would be an integral part of her journey and life's work. Understanding the

Human Experience, Eldership, the role, and importance of practical, natural healing and Wisdom, is a huge passion for Deborah. Through this she has created the unique 'Intrepid Soul Navigation System' which brings all the modalities she has studied, through the years and across the globe, together to help others uncover their true self, to reconnect with their inner wisdom and learn how to interpret their world, so they too can navigate life with ease.

As a Holistic Therapist and Speaker practicing and sharing her wisdom and knowledge around the world; she is based in Dublin and has clients in Ireland, the UK, Canada, the USA, Australia, and further afield. She has her own private practice where she sees clients in person and online.

You can contact Deborah J. Kelly and request her as a Guest Speaker, contact her for Guest Podcasting or Interviews, and you can work with her directly, by emailing her at deborahjsoulnavigation@gmail.com or check out her website www.deborahjkelly.com. You will also find her on Social Media as Deborah J. Kelly Intrepid Soul Navigation.

***

Printed in Great Britain
by Amazon

19022749R10081